EAR

10/08

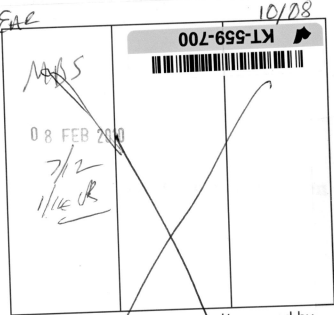
This book should be returned/renewed by
the latest date shown above. Overdue items
incur charges which prevent self-service
renewals. Please contact the library.

Wandsworth Libraries
24 hour Renewal Hotline
01159 293388
www.wandsworth.gov.uk Wandsworth

THE BRIGHTER BOROUGH

L.749A (rev.11.2004)

Faithful Conversation

*Christian Perspectives
on Homosexuality*

Edited by James M. Childs Jr.

Fortress Press
Minneapolis

FAITHFUL CONVERSATION
Christian Perspectives on Homosexuality

Copyright © 2003 Augsburg Fortress. All rights reserved. Except for brief
quotations in critical articles or reviews, no part of this book may be repro-
duced in any manner without prior written permission from the publisher.
Write: Permissions, Augsburg Fortress, Box 1209, Minneapolis, MN 55440.

Scripture quotations from the New Revised Standard Version of the Bible
are copyright © 1989 by the Division of Christian Education of the National
Council of the Churches of Christ in the United States of America and are
used by permission.

Cover image: *Group Chat*, © Diana Ong/SuperStock, 2001.
Used by permission.

ISBN: 0-8006-3580-9

The paper used in this publication meets the minimum requirements of
American National Standard for Information Sciences—Permanence of
Paper for Printed Library Materials, ANSI Z329.48-1984.

Manufactured in the U.S.A.
07   06   05   04   03   1   2   3   4   5   6   7   8   9   10

Contents

Contributors   vi

Foreword   vii
Conference of ELCA Seminary Presidents

Introduction   1
James M. Childs Jr.

1. The Bible and Homosexuality   19
Mark Allan Powell

2. The Lutheran Reformation and Homosexual Practice   41
James Arne Nestingen

3. Rethinking Christian Sexuality:
Baptized into the Body of Christ   59
Martha Ellen Stortz

4. We Hear in Our Own Language:
Culture, Theology, and Ethics   81
Richard J. Perry Jr. and José David Rodríguez

5. Talking about Sexual Orientation:
Experience, Science, and the Mission of the Church   97
Daniel L. Olson

Authors' Forum   121

Contributors

James M. Childs Jr. is professor of theology and ethics at Trinity Lutheran Seminary, Columbus, Ohio.

James Arne Nestingen is professor of church history at Luther Seminary, St. Paul, Minnesota.

Daniel L. Olson is professor of pastoral care at Wartburg Theological Seminary, Dubuque, Iowa.

Richard J. Perry Jr. is professor of church and society and urban ministry at Lutheran School of Theology at Chicago.

Mark Allan Powell is professor of New Testament studies at Trinity Lutheran Seminary, Columbus, Ohio.

José David Rodríguez is professor of theology at Lutheran School of Theology at Chicago.

Martha Ellen Stortz is professor of historical theology and ethics at Pacific Lutheran Theological Seminary, Berkeley, California.

Foreword

A wise pastor once noted that "Life is a dramatic mixture of brokenness and grace." Imperfect and forgiven, Christians live our callings in our homes and families, our work, our public roles, and our communities of worship. As the world and the church deal with various social, scientific, and personal interpretations of homosexuality, we in the Evangelical Lutheran Church in America are a community of faith seeking understanding, intent on bearing witness to the world of the hope that is ours in Christ Jesus.

Faithful Conversation contributes to the quest for understanding and exhibits our commitment to public witness. When the conference of seminary presidents commissioned this project, we knew that the questions are hard and the answers are disputed. Before the ELCA authorized the current studies in sexuality and prior to his current appointment as the director, we asked Dr. James Childs to gather faculty from our seminaries so that they could consult with each other on these difficult concerns and prepare a volume for the church. We expected that they would argue with each other just as other faithful Christians disagree among themselves. We also anticipated that these trusted teachers of the church would respect each other and know how to keep the unity we share in Christ Jesus at the center of their conversation.

Now we hope that you who read these essays will follow the examples of these teachers. On first reading, you may be eager to discover which essays make arguments with which you agree. Please stay in the conversation longer, perhaps especially with those essays with which you first disagree. You might not change your mind, but you might at least benefit from the differences brought together in one place and gain a new understanding of a point of view that is not your own.

All of these authors are seeking to be faithful to the witness of scripture. All of them are firmly opposed to all sexual promiscuity and infidelity. None of their cases are built on narrow notions of sexual freedom or personal rights. So also, none of them resorts to a simplistic literalism, as if the letter of God's law were God's final word.

Even some Christian practices change. To choose an easier example, the Apostle Paul declared that it is shameful for a man to cover his head in prayer or for a woman to pray with her head uncovered (1 Cor 11.4-5), but those disputes about what is or is not shameful do not divide the church in our time. The questions of sexual orientation or response patterns also do not threaten our unity. But we disagree on the boundaries of intimacy between members of the same sex. Many Christians also disagree on the boundaries of intimacy between members of the opposite sex, but the question at hand is that of homosexual relationships. How deeply divided are we?

Some Christians see almost all sexual intimacies among members of the same sex as immoral, even when the people involved are expressing their love and care in committed relationships. Other Christians regard the protection of such committed relationships as a matter of justice both in public and in the church. Some take their stand defending the sanctity of marriage between one man and one woman. Others intend to extend the circle of care and the security of intimacy to the homosexual sons and daughters of our families and to all whom Jesus Christ calls to faith. At their extremes, both groups are tempted to claim God's righteousness or God's mercy for their own views. Ultimately, only God's Holy Spirit joins righteousness and mercy in Christ Jesus. And at our best, all Christians will advocate God's law as a protection of the neighbor and the community.

As members of the ELCA conference of seminary presidents, we invite you, dear reader, into these *Faithful Conversations*. We do not know how our church will eventually address the questions of blessing same-sex committed relationships or the ordination of homosexual persons in committed same-sex relationships. We do not endorse everything written in these essays, but we are grateful for the courage and conviction of our faculty authors. We are heartened by their mutual confidence in the gospel of Jesus Christ, even as they sort many complex questions from several perspectives. We have learned from these teachers of the church. We pray for the counsel of the Holy Spirit for our church. May God's righteousness be accomplished among us forgiven sinners through God's mercy in Christ Jesus and for all people in the world God loves.

—Conference of ELCA Seminary Presidents
April 14, 2003

Conference of ELCA Seminary Presidents

President Michael L. Cooper-White
Lutheran Theological Seminary at Gettysburg

President James Kenneth Echols
Lutheran School of Theology at Chicago

President Philip D.W. Krey
Lutheran Theological Seminary at Philadelphia

President Duane H. Larson
Wartburg Theological Seminary

President Timothy F. Lull
Pacific Lutheran Theological Seminary

President Mark R. Ramseth
Trinity Lutheran Seminary

President H. Frederick Reisz
Lutheran Theological Southern Seminary

President David L. Tiede
Luther Seminary

Introduction

James M. Childs Jr.

The Evangelical Lutheran Church in America (ELCA), along with other
church bodies, is engaged in study and deliberation over the status of homosexuals in the life and work of the church. Currently, the ELCA encourages its congregations to welcome gay and lesbian persons as church members, but it does not allow for the approval or affirmation of gay or lesbian relationships. Specifically, the ordained, commissioned, and consecrated ministries of the ELCA are open to homosexuals only if they remain celibate, and no provisions exist for the blessing of same-gender unions.

The question before us is this: Should we continue with this approach, welcoming homosexuals into the life of the church while restricting their choices and activities? Or should we go beyond simply welcoming gay and lesbian persons and affirm them in their sexuality? Some are asking whether these are the only two choices. Conversation about such an emotionally charged and potentially divisive subject needs to be *faithful.*

First of all, our discourse must be *faithful to the mission of the church* to proclaim the gospel of Jesus Christ to all the world. The gospel creates and sustains the church, our Lutheran confessions tell us (Augsburg Confession VII), and sharing that good news is our holy calling (1 Pet. 2:9). Faithfulness in this connection means that our decisions should reflect a mindset consistent not only with our commitment to the gospel, but also with our commitment to preserving the unity of the church for the sake of its mission (Eph. 4:1-6).

Second, faithfulness means *faithfulness to the Scripture,* the Word of God, through whom we meet *the* Word, Jesus, the Christ, who is the grand finale of God's revelation in history. Listening to what the Bible said to those of its own day and discerning how this message speaks to the particularities of our day have been the perennial tasks of the church, pursued in its members' private study, in Christian education, in Sunday sermons, and in scholarly investigation.

Third, being faithful in our conversation requires a *faithful conversation with Christian tradition.* Lutherans understand themselves to be a part of the church catholic, professing the faith of the Christian community throughout time and

1

space. We regard our Lutheran confessions, assembled in the Book of Concord, to be a part of that tradition as well as a signal contribution of Lutheranism to the universal Christian community and a faithful account of biblical teaching. Being faithful, then, means maintaining continuity with Christian teaching in general and with our Lutheran theology in particular. At the same time, we recognize that theology must be done anew in each new generation. Faithfulness to tradition may not always mean repeating the same teachings in the same way. It may mean faithfully interpreting how the dictates of our faith apply in our peculiar situations, as our mothers and fathers in the faith did in their particular circumstances.

Finally, faithful conversation means being *faithful in engaging one another* in the sort of dialogue required to do justice to the serious issues of conscience involved in the consideration of homosexuality in the church. Perhaps the greatest temptation of all, when faced with a difficult subject, is to avoid the conversation altogether. For many in the church, discussions of sexuality are not comfortable to begin with. It is understandably difficult for some folks to get involved. Others believe that the Bible and the history of the church's teaching are plain on the subject. Therefore, they suspect that the mere fact of inviting dialogue is itself a betrayal of the faith because it suggests there might be something to talk about. Such suspicions, and the accompanying reluctance to talk, are understandable. Still others believe that the case for change is and has been obvious for some time. Conversation and study are only delaying tactics, they say. The church should be confronted with change now; gay and lesbian persons have been subjected to study long enough. Such sentiments are not hard to understand. There are more reasons too why people hesitate to talk to one another about these matters. However, the point is clear: there are obstacles to dialogue. Nonetheless, we are in this together and have a responsibility to care enough about each other to work at understanding one another's views and experience and to seek the truth together with the guidance of the Spirit, even if we may firmly believe we already know the truth.[1]

It is in the spirit of this vision of faithfulness that the presidents of the eight seminaries of the ELCA, in concert with the Division for Ministry of the ELCA, have commissioned this volume as a contribution to the discussion of homosexuality currently going on throughout the church. It is a modest contribution. Limits on the length of the book did not permit all seminaries to be represented. It also was not possible, with those space constraints, to treat all aspects of the discussion. Given the determination to enlist authors strictly from the seminary faculties, not all voices are being heard.

This set of essays is not meant to frame the discussion of homosexuality in the ELCA study process. That responsibility belongs primarily to the task force appointed by the church for that purpose. Therefore, it is most helpful to see this contribution as one resource and conversation within the larger churchwide dialogue. The essays collected here are not intended to be definitive, but helpful. Most important of all, they are written in a spirit of dialogue, not a spirit of debate. It is not a point-counterpoint exercise. These essays are slanted more toward service to the church's study and deliberation than toward advocacy for a specific viewpoint.

Readers may interpret the chapters' various authors as expressing a bias, but to the extent that that is true, their viewpoints are offered in the context of the kind of give-and-take dialogue that holds the greatest promise for mutual edification. No one comes to this discussion of homosexuality without some ideas and convictions. Even if they are uncertain about what the church should do regarding the blessing of same-sex unions and the ordination, commissioning, or consecration of persons in such unions, they will have some views on the sexual ethics of the Bible and Christian teaching. The key to a fair and faithful conversation is the readiness of participants to respect and listen as well as to propose and argue. That spirit of faithful dialogue pervades this volume. Although it arises out of a Lutheran context and speaks to that context, it is the sincere hope of the writers assembled here that their work will be useful to others who are asking similar questions in their own communions.

Faithful Conversations

Gearing up for faithful conversation will actually involve faithful conversations, plural. That is to say, there are various sources or focal points involved in discussing a Christian perspective on homosexuality, each of which requires its own "conversation," so to speak, and all of which must be discussed in relation to one another. These sources or focal points, as represented in the essays of this volume, are Scripture, tradition, culture, and (considered together) science and experience.

Perhaps these sources can be pictured as a Russian nesting doll. This kind of doll is really several figures, each encased in a larger one, as our sources are, and always involved with one another. Science and experience are inside culture, which is inside tradition, and all are surrounded by Scripture. So Scripture and tradition bulk larger than the rest, for they are the repositories of authority in the church's teaching. Tradition emerges from reflection on Scripture, but tradition is at the core of our understanding of the message of Scripture. Lesser in size, as influences and contextual factors rather than authorities, are culture and science and experience. (One might say "reason" instead of "science," since reasoning is always involved in theological and ethical formulation. However, for purposes of this topic, science is designated as a primary concern in view of the research efforts on the phenomenon of homosexuality.)

Scripture

For Lutherans the Bible is the Word of God, the center of which is the Christ. As Luther put it, the Bible is "the cradle of the Christ child." Lutherans further delineate the meaning of the conviction that Christ, the Word incarnate, is the heart of the Scripture by stipulating that the two basic doctrines of the Bible are the Law and the Gospel, which flower fully in the person and work of the Christ. Given this orientation to the Bible, it is clear that the paramount themes of Lutheran theology, drawn from the Scripture, will, in turn, guide Lutherans in their approach to understanding the Bible. It is helpful, then, that Mark Allan Powell's chapter, "The Bible and Homosexuality," provides an account of a Lutheran approach to the interpretation of Scripture, noting both distinctive Lutheran emphases and principles shared with most other biblical interpreters. Powell blends sound biblical scholarship and Lutheran evangelical sensibilities.

"Sound biblical scholarship" is a phrase to highlight, for the centrality of the gospel in a Lutheran approach to Scripture does not mean, to use Dietrich Bonhoeffer's well-known notion in a slightly new way, a "cheap-grace" reframing of what the texts say. This is evident in Powell's uncompromising recognition of the inescapably negative cast to the passages that speak directly of homosexual relations. Though he identifies, along with other biblical scholars, some of the uncertainties of these texts, he does not allow those uncertainties to provide an easy escape from the challenge posed by biblical judgments.

Powell alerts us to some of the ways in which some biblical scholars have questioned the continuing relevance of texts that speak against homosexual relations (page 30). Perhaps the most frequently argued point among these approaches is the assertion that the biblical writers had no conception of homosexuality as an *orientation,* such that what the Bible says must be reconsidered in the light of the contemporary understanding that, for some people, homosexuality *is* natural. Powell does not take this or any of the other paths mentioned, however. Rather, he chooses to take the biblical teaching at face value and still ask whether there are any exceptional circumstances in which the church might sanction homosexual relations within the parameters of the biblical witness.

Powell's analysis, which is better read carefully than summarized briefly, leads us to consider the possibility that the church might recognize some exceptions. It might be appropriate for the church to sanction some loving, exclusive, and committed gay and lesbian relations between persons who are set in their homosexual orientation and find that celibacy is not their gift. The biblical teaching that God wills no one to be alone might, in such circumstances, be allowed to counterbalance the biblical teaching that heterosexual marriage is the norm for intimacy. The language of "sanctioning" seems deliberately imprecise, though clearly it is not meant to be a synonym for marriage. Thus, he leaves open the question of how the church might proceed if it were to head in this direction. Powell's proposal bears some resemblance to suggestions made by others, but his analysis in dialogue with Scripture has its own distinctive features.[2] Even as he offers us this option for consideration, he is equally articulate in explaining why his ideas may still be unacceptable to some. He is more interested in prompting us to consider (and reconsider) what the God of the Bible would have us do than he is in stumping for a particular position.

Within the limits of one chapter, we have a laboratory for how one goes about understanding the biblical witness regarding homosexuality. Consistent with the general purpose of this book as a resource for the church's discussion, Powell does not debate a position or outline a policy but provides food for thought and one set of alternatives for dialogue.

As we leave this section on Scripture, let us recall the statement at its beginning: for Lutherans the Bible is Christocentric. As the dialogue within the church moves toward some form of resolution, the very Christ-centered character of this, our paramount authority, should tell us something of vital importance to the integrity of our faith. Whatever we in the Christian community do to impose discipline on ourselves should not be done out of fear. Whatever we choose to accept and allow should not be chosen out of mere tolerance or cultural pressure. Rather, in all such matters we should act in concert with what we know is the heart of our faith. We should act in the service of our call to witness to God's good news in Jesus Christ.

Tradition

Following the nesting-doll image, the next thing to emerge as we open up the Scripture piece is tradition. We are not surprised at this. The very observation just made about Christ as the focus and culmination of the Bible's narrative lays the foundations of the tradition that the two main doctrines of Scripture are law and gospel in correlation with one another, which in turn leads us directly to the Reformation's premier doctrine of justification by grace through faith. The teaching of Scripture informs the teaching of the tradition and the tradition keeps alive a clear understanding of Scripture as it develops a theology for faith and life that is faithful to the biblical message.

In his chapter, "The Lutheran Reformation and Homosexual Practice," James Nestingen gives us an exposition of a Lutheran theology for faith and life as it is revealed in the historical and confessional tradition of Lutheranism and as it has been developed in at least one prominent version of contemporary Lutheran social ethics. Applying this twofold account of Lutheran theology to the current discussion of homosexuality in the church, he provides a glimpse of the larger picture. His discussion of the Commandments, the use of the law, vocation, and the two kingdoms locates the concerns and purposes of sexuality in the context of our relation to God and our service to family, neighbor, and community.

Nestingen's account is not a mere summary of moral norms characteristic of the Lutheran and catholic Christian traditions, nor of their shared historical disdain for homosexual activity. That is acknowledged but not belabored. All matters are treated within the framework of justification by faith and the church's call to proclaim the forgiveness of sins in Jesus Christ. The result is an unfolding of the doctrine of justification as applied to matters of sexuality. It locates our ethical and theological outlook on sexuality within the context of that foundational teaching, without for a moment losing sight of its graceful core. The most challenging outcome of Nestingen's analysis will be noted later. The point for the present is that tradition, like Scripture, should be not only understood but applied. Nestingen has given us a good example of the process of understanding and applying.

Culture

Lurking within both Scripture and tradition is the influential reality of culture. Culture may be variously defined, but we generally think of it as a term covering the beliefs, concepts, habits, customs, skills, art, literature, and institutions that are the component parts of any given civilization. Culture is both the expression of and the bearer of the aspirations, hopes, projects, achievements, and failures of the human community in its efforts to build a world of meaning and purpose for life.

Scripture was written within the context of specific cultural realities. The language and concerns of the Bible reflect those various settings. Culture is the lens through which God's revelatory message is viewed and understood. This does not mean that the message is culturally relative in the sense of being obsolete or somehow unclear in our different cultural setting. Rather, it simply means that the interpreter's task is to appreciate the cultural form of the message in order to discern its substance for all time.

Cultural context is essential to appreciating the significance of the Lutheran reformation and its confessional writings. The manner in which the church dominated the culture of the time, the resulting confusion of politics and religion with its attendant forms of corruption, and the plight of Germany at the hands of Rome are but a few features of the cultural scenery for that theological drama.

Cultural changes impact the church's thinking and practice. The progress of science has, over the centuries, affected the church's reflections on the world of God's creation and on the culturally influenced way in which the Bible sometimes speaks of our universe. Cultural development can drive us to new understandings of the Bible. It is unlikely, for example, that we would have discovered the biblical foundations for women's ordination in the absence of a cultural movement on behalf of women's rights.

But even as culture may be implicated in positive changes, it can also be a corrosive influence, calling for a vigorous countercultural response from the community of faith. America's culture is highly individualistic, with a strong tradition of personal rights and freedoms. Many see this as the fertile ground from which has sprung a permissive society with very few moral sanctions, especially with regard to sexual conduct. While the breakthrough for women's ordination may be hailed as a great good, other proposed changes in response to cultural developments may not draw the same approval. Some would argue that proposed changes in our beliefs and practices regarding homosexuality are the result of culturally influenced pressures that should be resisted. Others who favor such changes might contend that it is a matter of not responding to cultural development but to demands of justice and truth that can be biblically defended.

Culture is the environment in which we live, and in today's world, to make matters more complicated, we recognize that American society is multicultural. We are aware that, though our country may have a discernable national culture, a variety of cultural traditions coexist within it. These have their origins in race, ethnicity, social location, religious belief, and so on. On the one hand, this cultural diversity represents theological riches: we see the many facets of God's Word reflected in the many cultures, as light is dazzlingly reflected off the many facets of a gemstone. In their chapter, "We Hear in Our Own Language: Culture, Theology, and Ethics," Richard J. Perry Jr. and José David Rodríguez note that positive aspect by reminding us of the "multicultural" Pentecost event. On the other hand, we fear that without agreed-upon norms all will be relative to different cultural biases and prejudices.

Culture as the product of human language and imagination is an aspect of the good creation. However, humanity is also sinful humanity and the products of its culture bear the marks of ambiguity. Impulses lofty and shallow, noble and debased, live side by side in human culture. The Holy Spirit embraced the multicultural reality of our world at Pentecost, reversing the confusion of Babel by a single unifying message of salvation and hope. However, in our multicultural world, where the influences of secularity too often seem to crowd out the message that the Spirit brought, many fear the return of Babel.

Given the inescapability of culture as our context and the ambiguity of culture's character, it is not surprising that the church has had a constant struggle on its hands with its relation to culture. Perry and Rodríguez call this to mind in their treatment of H. Richard Niebuhr's modern classic, *Christ and Culture.* Niebuhr charted the course of the church's deliberations over its relationship to culture throughout the ages and styled it as the "enduring problem." As Perry and Rodríguez point out, Niebuhr suggested that Lutherans accept the ambiguity of culture as our reality and understand God's will for our response to it in terms of Luther's doctrine of two realms.

Additionally, Perry and Rodríguez show that our newfound multicultural awareness can involve more layers of cultural complexity and ambiguity than we might have first imagined. Thus, for example, African American Christians, though sharing a particular cultural heritage of being Black in America, are still subject to the diversity of cultural pressures that affect us all. Therefore, cultural subsets within that community may take very different views on matters of sexuality due to the diverse influences of education, locale, economic status, and religious background.[3]

Awareness of the inescapable factor of culture, its ambiguity, its complexity, and our Lutheran orientation to these phenomena are essential components for understanding how to proceed with moral deliberation in the church. Additionally, Perry and Rodríguez alert us to the importance and benefit of learning from the efforts of nondominant cultures in our society as they engage the issues of sexuality we need to address.

Science and Experience

When we pop the lid off the culture "doll," the last figure to emerge in this discussion is that of science and experience. In many respects science and experience might well be considered part and parcel of the cultural context in which we operate. Indeed, that is what the visual image of the nesting dolls itself suggests. However, this twofold topic deserves separate treatment, especially in light of the debate about scientific studies in the discussion of homosexuality.

Whatever readers may expect under this topic heading, they will likely experience some surprises in Daniel Olson's chapter, "Talking about Sexual Orientation: Experience, Science, and the Mission of the Church." Olson first explores what behavioral science and human experience can tell us about the debilitating and denigrating effects of the sort of anger and mutual disdain that can easily erupt when a community becomes embroiled in a volatile issue such as homosexuality. His passion is for the teachings of Jesus that promote community and mutual respect and caring, even in the midst of controversy. Olson's concern is for the mission of the church and the importance of the way we treat each other to the strength of that mission witness. With particular reference to the present discussion of sexual orientation, he believes that it is our mission "to demonstrate to the world that it is possible, through the power of the Holy Spirit, to vigorously disagree about important, emotionally charged issues, without attacking one another in moral indignation, and without turning away from one another in moral disgust."

Olson draws on plenty of material from behavioral science to explore the unhealthy and often tragic consequences of anger. At the same time, he is always in touch with the Bible. His deft correlations between science and Scripture expand our appreciation of the relevance of biblical witness to our present concerns about homosexuality in the life of the church.

Olson moves on from his discussion of behavioral science and the deleterious effects of anger and disdain to a chastened account of what scientific inquiry can tell us about the causes of sexual orientation. The bottom line is that scientific investigation of the causes of sexual orientation and attendant questions about the effectiveness of change therapy, the mental health issues of homosexuals, and so forth, are by no means definitive in their conclusions. Therefore, we should be cautious when we see data from scientific studies used in debates, since their very inconclusiveness is often masked by those who seek to present that data in a way that favors their own convictions. In that observation there is a caution to all of us as we work with accounts of scientific inquiry. We should check out our own motives to be certain that we are after the truth and not yielding to the temptation to shape the data to fit our own truth.

Even though science has yet to isolate the cause or causes of sexual orientation, there has been a widespread acceptance of the scientific evidence that for self-identified homosexuals their sexual orientation is seldom a matter of choice. As a result, the ELCA and other churches have been welcoming of those of homosexual orientation but not affirming of homosexual sexual activity. Indeed, those who are willing to live the celibate life may even enter into the ordained, consecrated, and commissioned ministries of various church bodies. Since orientation is considered a given rather than a choice, moral culpability is not attached to it. However, homosexual *activity* does involve choice and therefore is subject to moral sanction. Pinpointing the cause of homosexuality with greater scientific certainty would not necessarily change the church's position.

Thus, the determination that homosexual orientation is a given, despite gaps in knowledge, is vital to acceptance of homosexuals at one level, but it has not brought the level of affirmation that some would desire. Again, greater scientific understanding would surely be valuable, but it would not settle the question of whether or not homosexuality is a natural variation in sexual orientation to be appreciated and affirmed in church and society.

The American Psychiatric Association decided in 1974 to remove homosexuality from its list of pathologies and has expressed its opposition to therapies aimed at changing sexual orientation. If these decisions could be shown without doubt to stand the scientific test of those who challenge them, it would advance the case for homosexuality as a natural variant for some but not for all.

But such scientific investigations, despite their importance, are not definitive in the life of the church. The status of homosexuality and homosexual activity is, finally, a theological question with ethical implications. Science can describe reality—to a greater or lesser degree—but theology (or philosophy in the secular sphere) interprets it within a framework of meaning and values. Placing the vexing issues of the day in the framework of meaning and values at the core of the Christian faith is central to the church's engagement in moral deliberation. It is a process involving all the "conversations" we have identified.

Moral Deliberation

The framework of meaning within which Martha Stortz would have us understand our sexuality and ourselves is our baptismal identity, our being Christian. This is our primary identity, within which we orient ourselves to our sexual orientation. As we engage in the moral deliberation associated with homosexuality and the church, Stortz proposes that we begin with baptism. Moral deliberation within the framework of baptismal identity means paying attention to the four sources involved in theological and ethical reflection: Scripture, tradition, reason, and experience. This traditional list of sources closely parallels the four focal points of the other chapters of the book. Here we gain a deeper sense of how they work together and what each of these sources might hold in store for us as we study and deliberate.

What Stortz has done for us is developed a sexual ethics for all Christians within the identity of baptism. As baptism involves promise keeping, so also our lives within the baptismal covenant we share as Christians, including our sexual lives, are marked by promise keeping. Such a notion means that our sexual relationships should be marked by the values of fidelity, service, and generativity that emphasize the larger communal dimension of life in the body of Christ. This is, by her account, a way of describing the lifestyle of discipleship. She believes that it provides us a sexual ethic that goes beyond simply forbidding certain actions to projecting positive values to which we can aspire by the grace of God.

Stortz does not want separate sexual ethics based on sexual identity. She wants one sexual ethic grounded in baptism and normed by the call to discipleship. Such an overarching sexual ethic for both heterosexual and homosexual relationships can readily be received as a formula equating both kinds of relationships in the practice of the church. That is a possible conclusion, but is it a necessary conclusion? That is open to further conversation. Stortz herself does not choose to engage the question of whether or not the church should ritually sanction same-sex unions.

Some forty years ago or so, Helmut Thielicke addressed the subject of homosexuality in *The Ethics of Sex*. He analyzed the phenomenon of homosexuality as an expression of a creation disordered by the Fall and contrary to God's original heterosexual design. Thus, he could not affirm the status of homosexuality per se. Consequently, for those whom Thielicke recognized as "constitutional" homosexuals, the optimum ethical course would be celibacy. However, if that is not their gift—it is the special calling of the relatively few—Thielicke proposed that such persons lead their lives in same-sex relationships in an ethically responsible way.

> In accordance with this conception we may assume that the homosexual has to realize his [her] optimal ethical potentialities *on the basis of* his [her] irreversible situation. Here one must seriously ask whether in this situation—naturally only in the case of adults!—the same norms must not apply as in the normal relationship of the sexes.[4]

While those who advocate complete affirmation of homosexuality would find scant comfort in Thielicke's view, others would find themselves very comfortable with it. They might deem his call for an ethic of responsibility, analogous to that of heterosexual marriage, as good and compassionate pastoral counsel. Interestingly enough, though, both perspectives could find much to embrace in the ethical account that Martha Stortz has offered as a means of renewing sexual ethics in the church.

Conversations and Deliberations

Discussing the matter of moral deliberation, as we just have, leads to some further thoughts about the fact that our faithful conversations definitely do involve serious deliberations. A resource for faithful conversation on homosexuality and the church needs to be alert to the sorts of deliberations that are involved. This kind of analysis could itself be a book-length endeavor. We cannot go that far, but we can at least unpack some of the deliberative exercises that seem to be involved in the church's discussion. For this purpose the nesting-doll image seems to work for us once again. Each of the following four items corresponds to one of the dolls, with the first being the outermost doll.

1. Conscience versus Conscience

Faithful conversation engaged in deliberation must recognize from the start that there are persons with divergent views who each feel conscience-bound to hold the position they do.

Martin Luther, appearing before the Diet of Worms, invoked conscience bound by the Word of God as the basis for his refusal to recant.

> Unless I am convicted by Scripture and plain reason—I do not accept the authority of popes and councils, for they have contradicted each other— my conscience is captive to the Word of God. I cannot and will not recant anything, for to go against conscience is neither right nor safe.[5]

In this well-known speech Luther says two things of importance about conscience, beyond the historical significance of his declaration. First, he echoes the long Christian tradition that, though conscience may err, one ought to follow one's conscience. It is wrong and dangerous to do otherwise, Luther says. Why? Because for Christians conscience is the deep sense of God's will that each has in faith. Second, he states that his conscience is bound to the Word of God. Conscience needs to be informed concerning God's will. The reliable source for that is Scripture, interpreted, we may infer from the quote, by plain reason.[6]

In today's circumstance the church is being asked to consider the blessing or sanctioning of same-sex unions and the admission of persons in committed same-sex unions to its ordained, commissioned, and consecrated ministries. Persons who support that move and persons who oppose it are, in many if not most instances, captive to conscience, based on their own reading of the Bible. To some extent their differences arise from disagreement on what certain texts say or how they should be interpreted in light of today's situation. To some extent differences are influenced by what portions or messages of Scripture should govern our perspective on the issues. Whatever the case, it is matter of how they see Scripture and "plain reason" shaping their consciences.

Because conscience can err, study and dialogue are needed, especially since *conscience* is *con* plus *scienta:* knowledge held in common and not just a matter of individual conviction. Because conscience must be respected, our deliberations require even more than the usual respect we owe one another as a matter of courtesy and Christian love.

Matters of conscience can be matters of moral discernment, but conscience can also involve articles of faith. Luther's speech at Worms dealt with profound and central concerns of gospel faith. Thus, when we open up the conscience versus conscience "doll," we discover another aspect of that deliberation lying in wait for us and yet another one within that.

2. Moral Judgment or Article of Faith
3. Decision and Division

Differences in moral judgment have always existed among Lutherans and in other Christian communions as well. For Lutheranism, as for other church bodies, disagreements over significant moral questions are serious but rarely church-dividing matters. For example, the Evangelical Lutheran Church in America has a social statement that expresses that church's position on abortion. Not all persons within the ELCA membership would totally agree with that stated position, but that fact has not caused congregations to leave the church body and form or enter new alliances. Similarly, the ELCA has a social statement that opposes the death penalty. There is division of opinion on this question as well, but not division of the church.

As volatile as questions of Christian teaching about homosexuality can be, no matter how we classify them, it would seem to make a difference whether we see them as moral questions or questions involving an article of faith. If we assume for a moment that the studies undertaken in the church, however edifying we hope they will be, will not produce widespread unanimity, it is important to explore the distinction between a moral judgment and an article of faith.

As a Christian community our moral judgments are rooted in the basic teachings of our faith. However, differences on a given moral issue may be tolerated if they involve disagreement over the interpretation of the facts involved and how the moral principles derived from our faith should be applied.

If the general belief is that some think homosexual unions are immoral and others don't, it may be possible to live with those differences. Changes in policy could occur without the church voting on what is moral or immoral or dividing

Growth in self-understanding by critically examining and clarifying our values and stances.

As editor, I am grateful to the authors of this volume for the dialogue in which they faithfully engaged as we went about our work. I know they join me in the hope that this modest effort will be a service to the church in its dialogue.

How to Use This Book

Our discussion of the ethics of dialogue provides a good backdrop against which to say a word or two on how people might use this book.

While viewpoints are discernable among the authors, this book is primarily informative, providing an account of many of the main considerations in the multidimensional discussion of homosexuality and Christian teaching. At the same time, readers familiar with this discussion in the church may find some new insights or be introduced to some aspects of the issues they had not been aware of before.

Though much ground is covered, not all ground is covered. Therefore, readers should and doubtless will see this volume as a contribution to the larger discussion of homosexuality in the church. The book takes its place among a vast number of resources available in print and other media.

The chapters have been written for a broad audience that includes students, pastors, and laypersons. Thus, the book should be suitable for use in classrooms, lay schools of theology, and a variety of discussion groups in congregations, as well as among pastors and other ministers of the church. This is a book designed to be discussed. The questions at the end of each chapter are there to help facilitate that conversation and study.

The best way to work through the volume is to read from start to finish. While each chapter can stand on its own, there is a logical progression in the arrangement of the chapters, with this introduction providing an overall orientation to the book as a whole.

Discussion Questions

1. Do you agree that the meanings of "faithfulness" given are a good definition of what *faithful* conversation involves? Are there other aspects of faithfulness that you would add? What must we do to make faithful conversation possible?

2. Reflect on scripture, tradition, culture, science, and experience. How do you think they have influenced the church's thinking on various issues throughout history?

3. How important should concern for the division of the church be in deciding about the blessing of same-sex unions and the ordaining, commissioning, or consecrating of persons in such unions?

4. Is dialogue as described possible in the discussion of these issues? If not, how do we proceed?

For Further Reading

Balch, David L., ed. *Homosexuality, Science, and the "Plain Sense" of Scripture.* Grand Rapids: Eerdmans, 2000.

Greenberg, David F. *The Construction of Homosexuality.* Chicago: University of Chicago Press, 1990.

Seow, Choon-Leong. *Homosexuality and Christian Community.* Louisville: Westminster John Knox, 1996.

Siker, Jeffrey S., ed. *Homosexuality in the Church: Both Sides of the Debate.* Louisville: Westminster John Knox, 1994.

Notes

1. The Bible provides an excellent example of the sort of deliberation that is required of us. In Acts 15: 1-19 we have an account of the "Apostolic Council" in which the apostles and elders, under the leadership of Peter and with the guidance of the Holy Spirit, were engaged in the heady question of whether Gentiles must be circumcised in order to be saved, as some contended. Adherence to dietary restrictions was also at issue. This is not to imply, as some do, that the decision of the council is a good analog for the decision to bless gay and lesbian unions and admit those in committed same-sex unions into the ministries of the church. It is, rather, an example of faithful conversation over a difficult matter.

2. Compare the discussion of "Position 4" in Patricia Beattie Jung and Ralph F. Smith, *Heterosexism: An Ethical Challenge* (Albany: State University of New York Press, 1993), 27–29.

3. Although space does not permit a global review of cultural diversity, it hardly needs saying that the church worldwide involves even more variations in cultural tradition as it affects issues of sexuality. In particular, with regard to homosexuality in the church, the lessons that the Anglican community learned at the 1998 Lambeth Conference of Anglican Bishops cannot be ignored. Clearly its vote to declare homosexuality as incompat-

ible with Scripture was largely due to the viewpoint taken by the numerically superior representatives from the third world.

4. Helmut Thielicke, *The Ethics of Sex,* trans. John W. Doberstein (New York: Harper and Row, 1964), 285.

5. As quoted in Roland H. Bainton, *Here I Stand: A Life of Martin Luther* (New York: New American Library, 1950), 145.

6. On Luther's conviction that the forming of Christian conscience requires not only the reading of biblical directives but their interpretation in the context of new and challenging circumstances, see Paul Althaus, *The Ethics of Martin Luther,* trans. Robert C. Schultz (Philadelphia: Fortress Press, 1972), 31–32.

7. An unpublished paper by James A. Nash, "The Character and Conditions of Dialogue: A Realist's Aspirations," 2002.

1.

The Bible and Homosexuality

Mark Allan Powell

Every reference in the Bible to sexual relations between same-sex partners is negative. Such relations are condemned as "unnatural" and "shameless" acts that result from "degrading passions." Accordingly, many Christians believe the will of God regarding such matters is obvious. They believe that Scripture presents homosexual relationships as sinful and that, accordingly, the Church should not bless or sanction homosexual behavior.

Many students of the Bible, however, do not believe the matter is so simple. At the time the Bible was written, the concept of "sexual orientation" was unknown; thus, some scholars believe the biblical passages often quoted as condemning homosexual behavior actually denounce homosexual acts performed by heterosexual people. Others believe that only specific instances of homosexual activity are condemned, such as prostitution, promiscuity, or sex with minors. Many Christians notice that no biblical text ever specifically comments on the morality of sexual relations between two men or two women who are in a loving relationship characterized by lifelong commitment. Thus, when two Christian men or women ask the Church to bless a relationship in which they will become romantic, spiritual, and probably sexual "life-partners," the Church is presented with a situation that never comes up, as such, in Scripture. What guidance does the Bible offer the Church in dealing with this issue and with related questions?

A Lutheran Approach to Scripture

Lutherans believe the Bible is the Word of God. We believe that God continues to speak to the community of faithful believers through Scripture and that what the Bible reveals about God's will is authoritative for our lives. Because we take the Bible so seriously, we try to study it for its true meaning rather than simply looking for verses to support what we already believe. To be authoritative in any real sense of the word, the Bible must be interpreted from a humble perspective that allows Scripture to inform and transform its readers' own viewpoints.

Lutherans (and most Christians) generally hold to some commonly accepted principles for interpretation of Scripture:

- Lutherans interpret Scripture *contextually*. We ask about the literary context of the book in which a passage is found and about the historical context of the situation it addresses.
- Lutherans seek to apply scriptural teaching to the present through a principle of *analogy*, asking whether situations in the modern world are comparable to those in the biblical world, even if they are not exactly the same.
- Lutherans interpret "Scripture in light of Scripture." This means that we try to reconcile what is said in one part of Scripture with what is said in other parts of Scripture, sometimes recognizing tensions between texts that seem to say different things. We try to be faithful to the entire Bible rather than choosing some parts and leaving others alone.
- Lutherans recognize that some scriptural points are more important than others. All of Scripture is the Word of God, but what the Bible says about loving one's neighbor is more important than what it says about picking grain on the Sabbath, and what it says about justification by faith in Christ is more important than what it says about speaking in tongues or eating food offered to idols. Jesus gives us principles for determining which matters are most important (e.g., Matt. 7:12; 22:37-40; 23:23) as do Paul (1 Cor. 15:3-4) and other biblical writers (Mic. 6:8; Heb. 6:1-2). The Lutheran confessions urge interpretation of all Scripture in light of "the gospel," the revelation of God in Jesus Christ that gives Scripture its true authority.
- Lutherans believe that the Church has the responsibility to determine the extent to which biblical teaching applies to the present day. Sometimes the Church has extended basic biblical teaching to cover matters not explicitly addressed in Scripture (e.g., modern Christians condemn slavery, which was permitted in biblical times). At other times, the Church has recognized exceptions to biblical teaching, specifying instances in which scriptural mandates no longer seem to apply (e.g., modern Christians save money for retirement in spite of Matthew 6:19-21, and women pray in church without head-coverings in spite of 1 Corinthians 11:2-16). In such cases, the Church bases its decisions on discernment of the will of God as revealed in Scripture as a whole.

A Biblical Overview of Sexuality

People are created by God as sexual beings and are encouraged to view their sexuality as a gift from God. The gift of sexuality is evident in at least three ways. First, sex normally allows people to participate in the divine act of creation and so to fulfill the divine call to "be fruitful and multiply" (Gen. 1:28). Two people who have been joined by God in a relationship of love (Gen. 2:21-25) are able to produce children who personify this union by embodying features inherited from both parents. Second, sex fosters intimacy, allowing two people to "become one" in a profound and mysterious way. The Bible warns that sex ought not be practiced casually, because sexual activity creates a durable bond between partners that is both emotional and spiritual (1 Cor. 6:15-20; Eph. 5:28-32). Third, sex is pleasurable. God intends people to enjoy sex, as is evident from the Song of Solomon and many other texts. The apostle Paul even counsels women and men not to deny their spouses fulfillment of their God-given desires for such pleasure (1 Cor. 7:3-5).

With regard to homosexuality, the first question that often arises is whether the Bible presents homosexual behavior as *unnatural* or *non-normative*. The short answer would probably be yes, it does, but such a claim requires further comment. For one thing, words such as "unnatural" and "non-normative" carry different connotations for different people. Some may use these labels to describe what they regard as "deviant" or "perverted" in a negative or even hostile way; others may use them simply to mean "atypical" or "nonconformist." Neither of these connotations would necessarily apply to the biblical perspective; the biblical writers simply viewed sex between a man and a woman as what God intended to be the "normal state of affairs." The creation story in Genesis indicates that God's design from the beginning was for a person to be raised by a father and a mother, then to form a new family with a person of the opposite sex and allow the cycle to be repeated (Gen. 2:24). Both Jesus (Mark 10:6-9) and Paul (1 Cor. 6:16; Eph. 5:31) refer to the Genesis story when asked about matters dealing with sexuality, affirming that they believe it presents God's intent. Thus, the argument that God creates or intends some people to be homosexual (just as God creates or intends other people to be heterosexual) finds no warrant in Scripture. From a biblical perspective, calling heterosexual unions the "normal state of affairs" does not just acknowledge heterosexuality as a dominant biological or cultural phenomenon but identifies heterosexuality as demonstrative of the original intent of God.

The Bible does not, however, automatically identify what is contrary to the "normal state of affairs" as evil or immoral. Consider the following:

- The Christian Church has understood Genesis as indicating that the "normal state of affairs" involves a man finding *one* woman and the two of them becoming one flesh. But Jacob (Gen. 29:21-30) and other biblical figures had multiple wives, and quite a few heroes of the Bible bore children by concubines (e.g., Abraham, Gen. 16:1-4). Although the Christian Church would come to regard polygamy as inappropriate for God's people, it would not condemn these instances of polygamy in an earlier time and place.

- The Christian Church has understood Genesis as indicating that the "normal state of affairs" is for a married man and woman to "be fruitful and multiply." But the Church does not view childlessness as an immoral failure to fulfill God's will. Even within the Bible, some couples (Chilion and Orpah; Mahlon and Ruth) never produce children (Ruth 1:1-5). Such childlessness may be regarded as unfortunate, but the childless couple is not viewed as sinful or wrong for not having kept God's commandment.
- The Christian Church has understood Genesis as indicating that the "normal state of affairs" is for a married man and woman to remain together until one of them dies (Matt. 19:3-6). Still, both Jesus (Matt. 5:32) and Paul (1 Cor. 7:15) allow for divorce in certain instances, and the Church has continued to recognize that such dissolutions must sometimes be permitted, even if they are contrary to what would have been God's original intent.
- The Christian Church has understood Genesis as indicating that the "normal state of affairs" is for people to find life-partners and marry (Gen. 2:18). Nevertheless, both Jesus (Matt. 19:12) and Paul (1 Cor. 7:8) claim that it is acceptable (even *preferable*) for some people to remain celibate and to have fulfilling lives as singles. Thus, the Church has celebrated celibacy as a gift of God and commended the single life for those who choose it.

In short, the Bible may be read as presenting a vision of what constitutes God's original design for humanity: monogamous, lifelong, childbearing unions between men and women. Nevertheless, the Bible does not indicate that every deviance from this projection is to be prohibited or condemned. Some situations that do not fit the "normal state of affairs" may be regarded as exceptional (polygamy) or unavoidable (childlessness). Others may be allowed as a "necessary evil" (divorce), and still others may be celebrated as the imposition of a higher calling (celibacy). Thus, it is at least *hypothetically* possible that some homosexual unions might be viewed as unnatural or non-normative in a sense that is not intrinsically derogatory. The Bible's vision of heterosexual unions as demonstrative of God's original design does not in itself rule out the possibility of the Church recognizing the legitimacy of some homosexual unions. The Bible itself, however, never articulates such an allowance—as it does with regard to the matters cited above—and the texts that denounce homosexual acts make the hypothetical allowance more difficult to justify.

Biblical Texts That Mention Sexual Relations between Same-Sex Partners

Only seven biblical passages mention sexual relations between persons of the same sex. Because of similarities, the seven texts are often discussed in four groups.

Genesis 19:1-9 and Judges 19:22-25

Two stories found in Genesis and Judges relate horrific tales of men who want to rape male visitors to their cities. In the Genesis account, angels disguised as men visit Abraham's nephew Lot in the city of Sodom, and a gang of violent men converges upon the residence with this intent. In the story found in Judges, a similar gang tries to assault a traveling Levite spending the night in the village of Gibeah.

Such stories reflect a mindset that regards the rape of men by other men as abhorrent, but with regard to current questions concerning homosexuality, these texts have little to offer. The stories speak only of the sin of homosexual rape and say nothing at all about consensual relations between persons of the same sex. The story in Genesis is later referred to in Jude 7, where the writer accuses the inhabitants of Sodom of being guilty of "sexual immorality" and of "going after other flesh" but, again, these descriptions probably refer only to the perverse character of abusive sex (and of men trying to have sex with angels) rather than to same-sex relations in general; in other biblical passages the Sodomites are castigated for failing to show justice to the poor and needy (Ezek. 16:49-50; cf. Isa. 1:10-17; 3:9-15). Thus, the stories in Genesis and in Judges have little relevance for matters that the Church is currently discussing.

Leviticus 18:22 and Leviticus 20:13

In two passages the Bible specifically prohibits sexual intercourse between male partners: "You shall not lie with a male as with a woman; it is an abomination" (Lev. 18:22); "If a man lies with a male as with a woman, both of them have committed an abomination; they shall be put to death; their blood is upon them" (Lev. 20:13).

These prohibitions seem unqualified and absolute. Some scholars have suggested that the restrictions were intended to prohibit participation in pagan fertility rites or to prohibit the sexual abuse that men might inflict on slaves, prisoners, or children, but they cite no good reason why the prohibitions would not also apply to other instances. We know from other texts (Deut. 23:17-18; 1 Kings 14:24; 15:12; 22:46; 2 Kings 23:7; Job 36:14) that male "temple prostitutes" associated with certain cults did exist, but nothing in the Leviticus passages limits the prohibition to acts involving such prostitutes. Likewise, the fact that *both* participants are to be punished (in 20:13) seems to imply that at least sometimes the prohibited sex was consensual. Indeed, these passages do not link the prohibitions to *any* particular motive or rationale: sexual intercourse between men is not condemned because it fails to produce offspring, or because it causes disease, or because it defies some ancient purity code, or because it undermines a patriarchal evaluation of men as superior to women (all of which have been suggested), or for any other discernible reason. It is simply prohibited, period, as activity that is an "abomination" to God. The one clue lies in the phrase "as with a woman," which occurs in both passages, suggesting that the act of homosexual intercourse is contrary to God's will because it involves a man doing something with another man that ought properly be done with a woman. This thought seems consistent with the perspective of the creation story: male-female intercourse is the normative expression of sexuality intended by God. But, as discussed above, while what is considered unnatural or non-normative is not *necessarily* regarded as wrong, the prohibitions here indicate that, in this case, it *is* regarded as wrong. In *these* texts, male-male intercourse is viewed not simply as exceptional or atypical but as "abominable."

There is nevertheless a significant problem with the Church using the two Leviticus passages to determine its position on homosexuality. Both passages are part of what is usually called the Holiness Code (Lev. 17-26), a block of material describing how the nation of Israel is to remain pure before God. While the material cannot simply be dismissed, the Christian Church has consistently taught that the Holiness Code is not determinative for Christian behavior or ethics. Many of the prohibitions (for example, against wearing clothing made from two types of material, or against planting two types of crops in a single field) may strike Christians as irrelevant, while others (against adultery, incest, and child sacrifice) reflect values still embraced within the Christian Church. The problem for interpreters is to discern which passages speak of what Christians should regard as enduring or universal standards and which reflect matters specific to the culture of Israel. Why should the Church make the prohibition against homosexual intercourse a part of its current moral code while ignoring the prohibition against a man and a woman having sexual intercourse during menstruation (Lev. 18:19; 20:18)? The traditional approach has been for the Church to identify the enduring moral commandments of Leviticus as the ones that are reiterated in later Scripture. Thus, the Leviticus passages should not be quoted on their own to establish a moral position for the Church, but they might be used to support such a position in combination with other texts.

1 Corinthians 6:9 and 1 Timothy 1:10

In two New Testament passages, the apostle Paul lists some of the types of people he regards as sinful, quoted here from the New Revised Standard Version with key words in Greek: ". . .fornicators, idolaters, adulterers, *malakoi, arsenokoitai,* thieves, the greedy, drunkards, revilers, robbers. . ." (1 Cor. 6:9-10); ". . . murderers, fornicators, *arsenokoitai,* slave traders, liars, perjurers . . ." (1 Tim. 1:9-10).

Some English Bibles (including the 1946 Revised Standard Version, which was widely used in Lutheran churches) translate these Greek words as "homosexuals," indicating that the latter are wrongdoers on a par with other types of sinners who need to repent of their wicked ways. Virtually no biblical scholar would defend such a translation today, especially since some people who call themselves "homosexuals" are celibate individuals who never have sexual relations with anyone.

No one knows precisely what the Greek words mean, but they do seem to refer to men who engage in sex acts with other men. The word *arsenokoitai* is extremely rare; in fact, it is found nowhere except in these two verses of Scripture and in later literature that probably depends upon them. Still, the word is a compound term formed from the Greek words for "male" *(arsen)* and "bed" *(koitai),* such that the resultant word ("male-bedder") could be a slang term for a man who "beds" (that is, has sex with) another man. The words *arsen* and *koitai* are both used in Greek translations of the Leviticus passages discussed above; accordingly, many scholars think that the term *arsenokoitai* refers generally to people who do what is prohibited in those texts. If this is true, then these two texts may function *together* with the Leviticus texts to extend the Holiness Code's condemnation of male-male intercourse as applicable to Christians. The texts interpret each other: the Leviticus texts give substance to the Pauline passages (indicating what *arsenokoitai* means), and the Pauline texts establish the continuing relevance of the Leviticus passages.

The word *malakoi* is not rare, but its meaning here is uncertain. The word itself means "soft," and Paul lists "soft people" here as sinners. In Greek literature the term is sometimes used as a slang expression for young men or boys considered weak or effeminate (for example, unfit for military service), and it sometimes denotes young men and boys who were used sexually by adult males. Since Paul here presents the *malakoi* as sinful persons, most scholars guess that the persons *he* calls *malakoi* were willfully engaged in such sexual relations and were not simply weaklings or victims of exploitation. Most scholars think that Paul uses the word as a counterpart to *arsenokoitai,* referring to effeminate males who allow other men to have sex with them.

Thus, Paul might be viewed as carrying the prohibitions from Leviticus over into the New Testament, indicating that they *do* apply to Christians: sexual intercourse between two men is regarded as sinful, and both the active *(arsenokoitai)* and passive *(malakoi)* participants in such activity need to repent.

Still, the Church must be careful not to base moral teaching on an unsure interpretation of Scripture, and these verses must not be allowed to carry more weight than they can bear. First, it is possible that the words are colloquial expressions referring to a particular type of homosexual conduct practiced in the first-century Corinthian culture (as opposed to homosexual behavior in general). Second, even if this is not true—even if the words *arsenokoitai* and *malakoi* were used to describe male-male sex in a generic sense—these words are certainly not technical or scientific terms that necessarily describe *any* instance in which a man engages in sex with another man. The word "fornicators" *(pornoi)*, also used in 1 Corinthians 6:9 and 1 Timothy 1:10, refers generically to unmarried people who engage in sexual relations. But the Christian Church has been willing to consider from time to time whether there might be exceptional circumstances in which sexual relations between persons who are not legally married might *not* be considered fornication. The same logic probably applies to all the words in these lists. The Church is able to denounce murder and stealing yet still engage in ethical discussions on possible instances in which a person who takes the life or property of another might *not* be a "murderer" or a "thief." If this is true with regard to common words whose meanings are relatively clear, it may be even truer for rare words and ambiguous slang expressions. In short, the condemnations of *arsenokoitai* and *malakoi* in these texts may imply that *generally speaking,* men who have sex with other men are acting in a way that is not pleasing to God, but such condemnations do not disallow instances in which men who have sex with each other are *not* behaving as *arsenokoitai* or *malakoi.* Thus, these texts do seem to speak against homosexual behavior, but they do not close the door on discussion of some of the questions that Christians have sought to ask. Condemnation of a certain kind of homosexuality in a particular context does not imply a necessary rejection of *every* expression of homosexuality in *every* context—nor does a *general* repudiation of homosexual acts preclude the possibility of exceptions.

The text from 1 Corinthians inspires further comment, because after listing examples of wrongdoers (including the *malakoi* and *arsenokoitai*), Paul says, "And this is what some of you used to be, but you were washed, you were sanctified, you were justified in the name of the Lord Jesus Christ and in the Spirit of God" (1 Cor. 6:11). The latter verse has become something of a "proof text" for those who wish to maintain that homosexuals can be changed or healed or even transformed into heterosexuals. The passage does indeed testify to the transforming power of God, but it seems to refer to changes in behavior rather than to changes with regard to what some modern therapists call a person's "sexual orientation." Still, even if the passage does not directly address the possibility of changing one's sexual orientation, it does indicate that God will sanctify those who repent of their sinful acts involving homosexual behavior (as well as those who repent of their sinful acts involving heterosexual behavior). The point is that God aids all those who repent, strengthening them to avoid the sinful conduct in which they once engaged. Nevertheless, the question remains: must all homosexual acts be considered sinful just because the acts associated with the first-century people known as *arsenokoitai* and *malakoi* were regarded as such?

Romans 1:18-32

In one fairly lengthy passage in the epistle to the Romans, the apostle Paul points to instances of same-sex intercourse as a prime example of behavior typical of people who reject God as their Creator. The key verses are found in Romans 1:26-27:

God gave them up to degrading passions. Their women exchanged natural intercourse for unnatural, and in the same way also the men, giving up natural intercourse with women, were consumed with passion for one another. Men committed shameless acts with men and received in their own persons the due penalty for their error.

The context for these verses is significant. Paul is writing to Christians in Rome and commenting in general on the "ungodliness and wickedness of those who by their wickedness suppress the truth" (1:18). He insists that such persons are "without excuse" because they defy what can be known about God from nature, from the things that God has made. His overall point seems to be that even people without Scripture to guide them should be able to recognize something of God's truth. Accordingly, those who do not possess the full revelation of God's will should at least live in accord with the truth that is available to all. But people have not done even this, as is evident from their penchant for idolatry: they worship images (1:23) and serve the creature rather than the Creator (1:25). As a consequence, Paul says, God "gave them up," allowing their rejection of the truth to have its full and logical effect. What does a world that rejects its Creator look like? Paul points to instances of homosexual relations as illustrative of such a world. Women and men alike do what is not "natural." They participate in acts of same-sex intercourse that Paul calls "shameful," driven by passions that he terms "degrading."

Some scholars have thought that Paul's ire is directed against something specific to the Roman context. Some have (again) proposed that the acts he refers to involve fertility rites performed with temple prostitutes, hence the connection to idolatry. Others have suggested that he is denouncing the goings-on at Roman orgies or sex parties, or even that he is protesting against a homosexual subculture in Rome, where a casual and promiscuous attitude toward sex was in fashion. It is also known, as indicated above, that same-sex intercourse was often practiced in exploitative ways in Roman society, involving minors, servants, or prisoners. But Paul does not object to what he calls "shameless acts" involving same-sex partners because they are promiscuous or exploitative; he specifically objects to them because they are "unnatural." That verdict would seem to apply to all instances of sexual intercourse between same-sex partners, regardless of whether the sex was casual and regardless of whether prostitution or exploitation was involved.

It should be noted that Paul is leading up to a broad declaration that *all* people have sinned and that, accordingly, his readers should not judge others (2:1) but recognize their own need for Christ's atonement (3:9, 21-25). He seems to mention same-sex intercourse because he wants to start the discussion with what he believes will be an obvious example. He expects his readers to regard "unnatural" sex acts between two women or two men as not only immoral but disgusting; once he has them hooked into condemning *those* sinners, he intends to move in and discuss some matters closer at hand (starting with 2:1). In other words, Paul is not primarily concerned with *establishing* that same-sex intercourse is wrong. He seems to take that for granted, and assumes that his readers do as well. His main point is to contend that the prevalence of such activity is only to be expected within a society that rejects God as Creator. When he says that those who do such things "receive in their own persons the due penalty of their error," he means that unnatural sexuality among unbelievers is an inevitable consequence of their rejection of God. The "penalty" is dishonor, a debasing of the self that is apparent to all who know what Paul calls "the truth of God." Thus, Paul regards these instances of same-sex intercourse not only as contrary to the will of God evident in nature but also as an ironic punishment. The people who rejected God as Creator no longer understand creation; they are even confused about the seemingly obvious fact that sex is supposed to take place between a man and a woman. As a result, they are now unwittingly dishonoring themselves in absurd ways that advertise their ignorance to the world.

Paul believes that humanity no longer functions the way that God intended. Ultimately, this goes back to what happened in the Garden of Eden and explains humanity's need for redemption (Rom. 5:12-19). Paul's point is this: the fact that people do such things—or even that they *want* to submit to "degrading passions" —demonstrates that God's original intent for creation is not being fulfilled. Paul's primary reason for pointing out the instances of same-sex intercourse in Rome is to show that because human beings rejected their Creator, the design of God has been distorted. Still, the people he describes as participating in these acts are not just victims of unfortunate circumstances. Paul wants to maintain that creation has gone awry while also indicting those who seem to celebrate the fact, willingly yielding to unnatural impulses.

Nevertheless, a possible distinction remains between what is unnatural and what is immoral or wrong. What is unnatural is not necessarily sinful, and sometimes what is unnatural must be accepted (divorce) or even encouraged (the adoption of children) as an accommodation to life in the world as it now is. In this Romans text, Paul seems to say that (1) *all* instances of homosexuality are unnatural; and that (2) the instances of homosexuality known to his Roman readers are *both* unnatural *and* wrong. This still leaves open the possibility of some instances (unlike what Paul describes) in which homosexual relations could be regarded *only* as unnatural but *not* as wrong. What might those be? Some theologians suggest that a committed relationship between two persons of the same sex, who have sought and received the blessing of the Church for their relationship, would fall into a very different category than what Paul is describing in Rome. Such relationships, they argue, might indeed be "unnatural" (in Paul's sense of the term), but they would not be sinful or wrong. We will consider this possibility below, noting, however, that the overwhelmingly negative portrayal of homosexual activity in the Bible places a heavy burden of proof on anyone who wishes to argue for exceptions to what appears to be a unanimous judgment of Scripture.

Repentance, Conversion, Celibacy

Thus far, we have outlined a biblical perspective that seems to support repudiation of all sexual activity between persons of the same sex. The Bible indicates that God's intention at creation was for heterosexual relationships to constitute the "normal state of affairs" in human society. That which is contrary to the normal state of affairs is not *necessarily* sinful, but the Holiness Code in the book of Leviticus indicates that homosexual activity is unnatural in a way that *is* sinful. Not everything in the Holiness Code applies to Christian morality, but Paul's apparent citation of the prohibitions against same-sex activity (through use of the word *arsenokoitai*) carries those commandments over into the New Testament in a way that *does* make them relevant. Furthermore, in Romans, Paul refers to same-sex relations between either male or female partners as a prime example of conduct that marks a society alienated from God.

The matter becomes complicated somewhat when we ask a question that the Bible never specifically addresses: What should these people who are engaged in sexual activity with same-sex partners be doing instead? In the modern Church, two suggestions are typically offered: a) they should reject homosexual relationships in favor of heterosexual ones, or b) they should remain celibate. The biblical witness favors the first of these. The texts discussed above tend to present heterosexual relations as the alternative to sinful same-sex couplings: "lie with a male *as with a woman*" (Lev. 18:22; 20:13); "men, *giving up natural intercourse with women,* were consumed with passion for one another" (Rom. 1:27). The implication seems to be that persons who engage in such activity ought to find sexual fulfillment more properly in heterosexual marriages. But what if such marriages are not a realistic option? The latter question never comes up in the Bible but is often asked today in light of a modern understanding of "sexual orientation." In our present context, the majority of people who engage in sexual activity with same-sex partners identify themselves as homosexual in *orientation* and thereby as persons for whom heterosexual marriage would be inappropriate. What should *these* persons do, if they are unable to find sexual fulfillment in heterosexual marriage but are also prohibited from forming intimate relationships with same-sex partners?

The quick answer of the Church has been, "They should remain celibate," that is, deny themselves participation in sexual relationships altogether. This may be the best possible response (we will discuss it further below), but it is not without problems biblically. Jesus says that celibacy is something that "not everyone can accept . . . but only those to whom it is given" (Matt. 19:11). Paul likewise allows that many who are encouraged to celibacy will find themselves "aflame with passion" (1 Cor. 7:9) in a way that is neither healthy nor pleasing to God. Thus, the Bible seems to present lifelong celibacy as a higher calling that people should be encouraged to seek but not as an obligation that can simply be imposed on people. This point, incidentally, is strongly echoed in the Lutheran confessions, which maintain that apart from "a high supernatural gift," it is *impossible* for a person who is required to remain celibate to please God (see the Sixth Commandment in the Large Catechism and Article 23 in the Apology to the Augsburg Confession).

It may be instructive at this point to consider the reasons why the Lutheran church has traditionally interpreted Scripture as opposing lifelong celibacy requirements. The resistance to such requirements is strong in the Lutheran confessions, which maintain that any rule that insists on lifelong celibacy "clashes with divine and natural law, endangers religion and morality, and produces endless scandals, sins, and the corruption of public morals" (Apology to the Augsburg Confession, 23.6). Why? First, there seems to be a strong suspicion that many who try to remain celibate will fail. They will yield to temptation and fall into sexual sin. This seems to represent the thinking of Paul in 1 Corinthians 7:37, but it is ultimately only a minor concern. Jesus calls all people to practice self-denial, and Paul promises that self-control is a fruit of the Spirit (Gal. 5:22-23). With God's help, and with support from the Church, celibate people (including gays and lesbians) can no doubt learn to keep their sexual appetites in check. A wider concern is that even those who succeed at maintaining their virginity may be consumed by what the Bible calls "lustful passions" and be forced to devote an inordinate amount of spiritual energy to managing that one area of their lives. So the Lutheran confessions maintain that "impure continence does not please Christ" (Apology to the Augsburg Confession, 23.22; cf. the Large Catechism, 6.215).

But there is yet another sense in which celibacy requirements render a person's life displeasing to God. The person upon whom such a requirement is imposed is denied not only fulfillment of sexual desires (a relatively small matter) but also the experience of intimacy and love that sexuality is intended to express. When a person is told, "You must remain celibate," he or she is not simply being told, "You cannot have sex with anyone." The requirement implies much more than that. It implies, "You cannot have a spouse—a lifetime partner with whom to share your life and 'become one.'" It implies, "You cannot experience the joys of marriage and all the attendant blessings of married life." It may even imply, "You cannot know the thrill of romance and the joy of romantic love." In effect, when a person is told, "You must remain celibate," he or she is being told, "You must live your life in a way that God says is 'not good'" (Gen. 2:18). Thus, the Lutheran confessions are scripturally sound when they affirm that a human being's life will not normally be pleasing to God when that person is required to remain celibate. Why? Because God says it is not good for a human being to "be alone," to miss out on the fullness of life experienced by becoming one with another. Of course, celibate persons need not be completely alone—they may have friends and companions and they may discover a substitute family through fellowship with their brothers and sisters in Christ, but such relationships do not necessarily meet the basic human yearning for an intimate, lifelong relationship through which two persons may be said to "become one" (Gen. 2:21-24).

We should emphasize that the "not-goodness" of such a life is a matter of degree, and biblical teaching that exalts marriage should not be read as disparaging the single life. First, there are single people (perhaps those with the "gift" of celibacy) who are more satisfied and fulfilled than they would be with a partner. Furthermore, not all who have been unable to find a partner in life are utterly miserable; some may experience the lack of a desired relationship as only a mild disappointment. In the latter case, the point may be simply that one *aspect* of the person's life is "not good," or at least not as good as it could be. Perhaps, then, gay and lesbian people should be encouraged to live as celibate, single adults who sublimate their desires for sexual relationships and find fulfillment in other aspects of life. But there are significant differences between (a) an individual who chooses to live as a single person, (b) an individual who would prefer not to live as a single person but who is unable to find a partner, and (c) an individual who is *required* to live alone when otherwise he or she would find the partner he or she desires. These are distinct categories, and the Church must think carefully about whether it really wants to require people to live in a manner that its Scriptures and its confessions maintain is displeasing to God. But are there any other options?

In Romans, Paul explicitly identifies those engaged in what he considers "shameless" sexual acts with same-sex partners as persons who have rejected God (1:24-25). What, then, should a homosexual person who does not reject God do? It seems unlikely that Paul would have counseled a homosexual believer simply to remain celibate, to spend a lifetime striving for control of passions analogous to those that he thought would be the undoing of heterosexual believers (cf. Rom. 1:27 and 1 Cor. 7:9). More likely, Paul would have hoped that the sanctification of a believer by Christ and the work of the indwelling Holy Spirit would remove the "degrading passions" for same-sex intercourse and replace them with natural yearnings that would allow for a normal, heterosexual marriage (Rom. 6:22; 1 Cor. 6:11). But if that did not happen, then what? Some theologians argue that Paul would not want his remarks about the disgraceful sexual antics of godless Romans to be used to force some Christians into a life devoid of the familial blessings that God willed for all creation (Gen. 2:18). Others insist that Paul never would have "caved in" on this matter; he would have favored excommunicating Christians who engaged in homosexual activities just as he did believers who were involved in incestuous relationships (1 Cor. 5:1-5). But all of this is speculation: we cannot know for certain what Paul would have prescribed for the redeemed Christian who continues to have homosexual impulses or who engages in homosexual activity that is neither promiscuous nor exploitative. In any case, no projection of what Paul "might have thought" about this situation can be determinative for the Church's deliberations. Canonical authority extends only to what is actually written in documents that the Church confesses to be Scripture, not to what thoughts the authors of those documents might have entertained but did not record.

Summary of Biblical Teaching

The Bible does not tell us everything we need to know about this topic, but it does tell us quite a bit, and the Church must be attentive to what Scripture says. We can affirm the following descriptions of biblical teaching as potentially relevant for the current debate:

- The Bible teaches that it is the will of God for all people to have the opportunity of sharing life with a partner, a person with whom they form an intimate bond so as to "become one." However, the Bible appears to indicate that such bonds are to be formed between men and women, not between two men or between two women. The Bible consistently presents heterosexual relations as the "normal state of affairs" in keeping with the original design of God at creation; homosexual relations are regarded as a departure from God's design.
- The Bible never mentions the phenomenon of homosexual *orientation* as such. The Bible deals only with homosexual *acts*. References to such acts are few and somewhat ambiguous, but *all* references to sexual activity between persons of the same sex are negative.
- The Bible offers little counsel on what homosexuals who believe in Jesus Christ ought to do if they are to live as God intends. Some persons who once engaged in sexual acts with same-sex partners may be transformed and do so no longer (1 Cor. 6:11). Otherwise, celibacy is to be encouraged but, if required, will render many people's lives "not good" in the eyes of God.

Interpretation of the Bible for Today

Thus far, we have focused on describing the teaching of the Bible concerning homosexual behavior, on articulating what the Bible does and does not say. Even those who agree on "what the Bible says," however, may disagree on the significance of this perspective for present-day discussions. Some theologians question the relevance of biblical teaching on this subject altogether. The following arguments have been made but will not be discussed here:

- Some have said that the biblical writers' views on same-sex behavior must be discounted because they did not understand sexuality as we do today. According to this view, the biblical writers did not realize that some persons are homosexual in orientation (possibly from birth or as a result of genetic predisposition) so that what is "unnatural" for heterosexuals is perfectly natural for homosexuals.

- Some theologians do not want to limit our understanding of God's creation to what is revealed about an "original design" in Genesis. They maintain that creation should be understood as an ongoing process so that variations (including the diversification of races and, possibly, the variety of sexual orientations) developed over time in ways consistent with God's intent.

- Some theologians contend that the Bible is not immune from the prejudices of the human beings who wrote it. The (heterosexist) perspective that privileges heterosexuality as normative, they argue, is analogous to the patriarchal perspective that regards men as intrinsically superior to women. To them, this is an unfortunate prejudice that must be corrected if God's truth is to emerge from the cast in which it was set by biblical authors unable to transcend their own cultural limitations.

- Some theologians maintain that recognition of biblical authority involves only acceptance of what the biblical authors intended to teach, not necessarily of the *assumptions* they might have held. They maintain, for example, that biblical authors may have assumed that the sun revolves around the earth (Josh. 10:12-14) but that no biblical writer teaches us to believe this. Likewise, they might argue that Paul merely *assumed* that homosexual conduct is sinful without intending to *teach* this. The point Paul intended to make in Romans was that all humanity is sinful—and this can be accepted apart from specific assumptions evident in his argument.

All of these arguments deserve to be heard, but they will not be considered further in this particular essay. Our (limited) focus is on how a Church that *does* accept the relevance of the biblical perspective, as described in the preceding section, might interpret the biblical material for contemporary situations. The question, then, becomes one of *application:* do the biblical prohibitions against homosexual conduct apply to present-day circumstances, and could there be exceptional instances to which they would not apply?

Application of ethical demands in Scripture always requires discerning two possibilities: first, that specific directives given in one context might apply more broadly to other matters in other contexts; and second, that certain circumstances might allow for exceptions to what would usually be expected. Thus, some Christians interpret the command "Thou shalt not kill" broadly to prohibit abortion, but even those who claim abortion is wrong sometimes recognize particular cases in which it should be allowed (for example, when a mother's health is endangered). Or, again, some Christians interpret "Thou shalt not kill" broadly to prohibit participation in warfare, but even those who hold this view sometimes make allowances for specific circumstances (arguing over what constitutes a "just war"). Discussions of *application* of Scripture to modern life can be controversial among people who all agree on the validity and authority of the Bible itself. Accordingly, we should emphasize from the outset that these are matters on which good and faithful Christians will disagree.

With regard to the issue of homosexual behavior, questions of the first sort—applying directives more broadly—seem to be only a minor concern. Some interpreters have suggested that the injunctions against unnatural relations for homosexual couples should be extended to include the prohibition of unnatural intercourse (for example, oral and anal sex) for heterosexual couples as well. If the concern is to avoid any sexual activity that is "unnatural," such logic probably applies, but so far this argument has not attracted much attention in the current debate. The greater controversy concerns the question of whether the Church should recognize any exceptions to the general prohibitions.

This question arises out of contemporary experience. In recent years, thousands of homosexual Christians have asked the Church what they should do to have lives that are meaningful, fulfilling, and pleasing to God. As the Church has struggled with this issue, it has come up with answers that seem to provide only partial solutions. For instance, some Christians have endorsed therapy programs intended to enable homosexual persons to change or to transcend their sexual orientation. The advisability and effectiveness of such programs is contested, but for our purposes we need only note that even the most enthusiastic advocates of such programs claim a success rate of about 30 percent (or, indeed, about 30 percent of those who seek help early and who meet other criteria for such treatment). Thus, by any account, a large number of persons remains. The Church has typically advised these individuals that they must remain celibate, refraining from all sexual activity. As indicated above, both the Bible and the Lutheran confessions contend against the practical effectiveness of such advice for all but a few, and experience has borne this out. Thus, the Church is left with thousands of homosexual Christians for whom neither therapy nor celibacy appears viable. They experience what Paul calls "burning" for a life-partner, but the option Paul recommends for such people, marriage, is not available to them. They want what most humans want—to fall in love and to form a family with one special person—but the Church says that what seem to them to be natural desires are denigrated in Scripture as "degrading passions." When they seek to obey what seems to be the teaching of the Bible (and the Church), they discover that their lives nevertheless fit a pattern that God explicitly calls "not good" (Gen. 2:18). And so they turn to the Church again and ask, "What should we do?"

This is the context in which the Church must consider possible exceptions to the biblical prohibitions against homosexual behavior. Merely raising the question of whether there *can* be exceptions to what the Bible teaches may at first seem irreverent ("looking for loopholes") or impudent (resistance to biblical authority), but we are actually encouraged to raise such questions by the biblical writers themselves. In the Gospel of Mark, Jesus seems to prohibit divorce for *any* reason (Mark 10:2-12), but in the Gospel of Matthew, he allows for one exception: when the spouse has been unfaithful (Matt. 5:31; 19:9). The apostle Paul would allow for another exception: an unbelieving spouse who will not consent to living with a Christian (1 Cor. 7:15). As time went by, the Church would permit divorce for many other reasons as well, with the understanding that the continuance of a bad marriage can constitute a worse state of affairs. Likewise, in remote locations where neither clergy nor legal magistrates are readily available, the Church has sometimes allowed committed couples to form sexual unions and bear children without taking part in a civil marriage service. Even today, the Lutheran church (like other denominations) allows for polygamous marriages among the Maasai people in East Africa, where such relationships are integral to social structure. In the latter instance, the church continues to regard monogamous relationships as normative so that allowing for the exceptional character of some Maasai marriages does not compromise the integrity of the church's ideals. The church encourages the Maasai toward monogamy, but if a Maasai man with multiple wives becomes a Christian, he is not directed to divorce his spouses; indeed, he is encouraged to remain married to all of his wives and to continue to engage in sexual relations with all of them.

Should the Church grant such an exception for homosexual couples who are committed to a lifelong relationship? The question remains controversial. As indicated above, the Bible presents sexual activity between same-sex partners as intrinsically unnatural but not as intrinsically sinful. Still, in the biblical writings themselves, sexual activity between same-sex partners is consistently regarded as both unnatural and sinful every time it is mentioned. In other words, while the *possibility* of some type of nonsinful sexual activity between same-sex partners is not ruled out, such a possibility remains completely hypothetical within the Bible itself. Thus, a heavy burden of proof rests on those who want to claim that certain instances of homosexual behavior in the modern world qualify for such exceptional status.

The simple demonstration that same-sex couples are able to form loving, committed relationships is not sufficient. The mere fact that a stable family unit can be established offers no carte blanche for ignoring biblical teaching on sexual ethics. Most people would oppose the Church permitting someone to continue in an incestuous relationship even if the partners demonstrated positive qualities of mutual love and fidelity (cf. 1 Cor. 5:1-5). But, then, people involved in incestuous relationships do not usually maintain that they are so incest-oriented that a meaningful nonincestuous sexual relationship would be impossible for them. The pressing point for the Church with regard to homosexuality occurs over this issue: if there are persons in the Church and in the world at large who cannot find fulfillment of their God-given desire for an intimate life-partner through heterosexual relationships, is it God's will for them never to find such fulfillment at all? Or would it be better for them to fulfill that yearning for a life-partner through a bond that might seem unnatural and even "degrading" to traditional Christians but is nevertheless satisfying to the couple themselves?

The question is *not* "Should the Church allow persons who have homosexual urges to gratify those desires by engaging in sexual acts with persons of the same sex?" That would be a fairly easy question to answer. The Bible never says that it is God's will for people to be able to gratify all of their sexual desires; in fact, Christians are encouraged to control their desires and to deny themselves gratification of those desires that constitute temptations to sin. The Bible does indicate, however, that it is God's will for individuals to have the opportunity to share their lives with intimate partners (Gen. 2:18-25). The Church may set limits regarding such partnerships (prohibiting marriage to close relatives and discouraging marriage to unbelievers), but to insist on limits that deny thousands of people the possibility of such relationships altogether is to fly in the face of Scripture. Even while paying heed to the Bible's prohibitions against same-sex intercourse, the Church also must recognize God's clear declaration that it is not good for a person to have to live life alone.

The Decision before Us

A major decision that the Church now faces is whether to sanction (that is, to allow or, possibly, to bless) some relationships between some homosexual persons who meet certain criteria defined by the Church (for instance, public commitment to a lifelong monogamous union). Before summarizing the biblical arguments that might be used to oppose or sustain such a decision, let us clarify what the Church would *not* be doing in granting such allowances:

- The Church would not be endorsing homosexuality as an alternative lifestyle that Christians may or may not engage in as they wish. The Church could continue to respect the biblical perspective that regards homosexuality as a departure from God's original design and that presents homosexual behavior as activity that is normally contrary to God's will. It is not necessary for the Church to question such propositions to recognize that certain circumstances may justify exceptions to the usual policy.
- The Church would not be redefining marriage as a partnership that may be constituted by same-sex couples as well as by heterosexual ones. The Church could continue to affirm its traditional understanding of marriage and recognize certain homosexual relationships as something other than marriage—as relationships that have value in their own right but that do not constitute actual marriages.
- The Church would not be endorsing or even condoning any specific sex acts that might be performed by same-sex couples. Homosexual male

couples do not all engage in anal and/or oral sex, and many lesbian couples say that they never engage in sexual activity that leads to orgasm. The Church would focus, at any rate, on recognizing the legitimacy of *relationships,* not on recognizing the legitimacy of sex acts. Accordingly, Christians within the Church might continue to question the legitimacy of certain types of homosexual activity even if the Church as a whole affirms the intimate (and, indeed, sexual) nature of some homosexual relationships. This, of course, would be in keeping with the Church's stance toward heterosexual relationships, whereby the blessing of a relationship (through marriage) does not imply a blanket approval of every sexual act in which the two persons might choose to engage.

- The Church would not be rejecting or discrediting the views or efforts of those who encourage celibacy or therapy as "first options" for gay and lesbian persons. Though some persons in the Church might oppose those options and celebrate homosexual partnerships with the same enthusiasm that attends heterosexual marriages, others might view such partnerships more as a tolerable "last resort" to be instituted only when celibacy and therapy have failed. The Church could acknowledge such diversity without any official ruling as to who is right and who is wrong. In any case, a decision by the Church to sanction some homosexual partnerships would only create another option for some gay and lesbian persons; it would not nullify any of the options that are currently available.

Even with these qualifications, however, a decision to sanction intimate relationships between same-sex partners would be a controversial one. The Church must now weigh two opposing concerns, both of which have validity in scriptural teaching: On the one hand, the Church must recognize that the Bible regards the instances of same-sex intercourse to which it refers as shameful and degrading acts, unacceptable conduct for God's people. On the other hand, the Church must recognize that God does not want homosexual persons (or anyone else) to have to live alone, denied the opportunity of "becoming one" with a life-partner through an intimate bond of love and devotion. Still, the issue is not so simple as choosing one part of the Bible and dismissing another. The goal is to be faithful to all of Scripture.

We may imagine a spectrum of "biblically consistent views" according to which persons reach different conclusions in light of the weight they assign to different factors. Key points in the debate seem to be (1) the degree to which the lack of a life-partner deprives one of experiencing life in a way that God would call "good," (2) the extent to which a homosexual partnership may be understood as approximating the sort of intimate (normally heterosexual) bond that God willed to be a part of human experience, and (3) the latitude with which the Church can recognize some expressions of homosexual love in contemporary relationships as distinct from acts that would violate the intent of the biblical texts denouncing same-sex relations.

At one end of the spectrum, we might find a Christian who thinks that

- the absence of an intimate partner in life, while unfortunate, need not render one's life altogether tragic;
- an intimate relationship with a same-sex partner offers, at best, a poor substitute for the sort of connection obtained through heterosexual marriage;
- the biblical texts are so uniform in their condemnation of homosexual acts as to make the granting of any exception for any reason almost unthinkable.

Such a person would not be likely to favor the Church's sanctioning of any gay or lesbian relationship but would instead take the view that homosexual persons should learn to make the best of things and, with God's help, learn to have meaningful lives as single, celibate individuals.

At the other end of the spectrum, we might find a Christian who thinks that

- a person required to remain celibate is forced to miss the very aspects of life that many consider to be most precious (romance, marriage, sex, family);
- a committed and loving relationship between two same-sex partners allows homosexual persons to come much closer to experiencing such aspects of life than they would otherwise;
- the biblical texts that condemn homosexual acts are so geared toward regulating sexual *preferences* that their application to persons of homosexual *orientation* is a matter that merits special consideration.

This person would be likely to favor some sort of Church action to allow for the sanctioning of at least some gay and lesbian relationships: homosexual persons should be allowed to enjoy life at its best in responsible ways, remaining accountable to God and to the Church.

Personally, I recognize the pros and the cons of both arguments and strive to avoid adoption of either extreme. Still, I believe that Jesus urges us to resolve difficult matters with a bias toward mercy and compassion. For me, the question becomes: Do we require homosexual people to sacrifice the experience of sharing life intimately with a partner in order to fulfill God's standards of holiness as perfectly as possible? Or do we allow a merciful exception to those standards in the belief that God would not want such sacrifices imposed on people in burdensome and harsh ways (see Matt. 11:28-30; 23:4)? The Bible prizes both sacrifice and mercy but teaches that God *prefers* mercy to sacrifice (Hos. 6:6)—a principle that Jesus himself quotes more than once (Matt. 9:13; 12:7). I cannot help but recall Jesus' treatment of the biblical law prohibiting work on the Sabbath (Exod. 20:8-

11), which he interpreted in light of the fact that "the Sabbath was made for humankind, and not humankind for the Sabbath" (Mark 2:27). The purpose of the law prohibiting work on the Sabbath, Jesus contended, was to enhance human life, not make it burdensome. The law itself was good, but when it was applied in ways that actually prevented people from enjoying God's blessings, Jesus was quick to allow exceptions to it. In the same way, I believe that the Church should not dismiss or ignore biblical teachings against homosexual relations but that the Church should follow the lead of Jesus in recognizing that exceptions must be granted in some instances to enable homosexual people to experience life as abundantly as possible.

In closing, we should remember that Jesus also singled out two commandments—love for God and love for neighbor—as more important than all the rest. Indeed, these commandments hold the key to interpreting all others, such that Jesus could say that everything required by the law and the prophets depends on these two commandments being observed (Matt. 22:40). This means, for instance, that homosexual Christians should not approach questions regarding their sexual conduct with an attitude that asks "What am I allowed to do?" or "How much can I get away with?" The question, rather, ought to be "How can I please God, whom I love and want to serve?" Thus, homosexual Christians who ask the Church to bless an intimate and potentially sexual relationship should only do so with a sincere conviction that they will be able to serve and love God best within such a relationship. Likewise, the Church as a whole should not be concerned with enforcing rules for their own sake but with interpreting commands in ways that promote love for God and neighbor. All Christians are expected to love gay and lesbian persons as their neighbors and to want them to have meaningful and satisfying lives. The issues involving homosexuality are difficult, but they need not be divisive among those who are willing to subject their own opinions to the scrutiny of Scripture and who are motivated by an overwhelming love for God and for one another.

Discussion Questions

1. How important is it to you that the Bible seems to present homosexual relationships as "unnatural" or contrary to what the author calls "the normal state of affairs." Does this mean that such relationships are immoral and always to be avoided?

2. The author says that although the Bible contains several passages that speak negatively about homosexual acts, it never indicates what homosexuals who want their lives to be pleasing to God should do. Should they find heterosex-

ual partners? Should they commit themselves to lifelong celibacy? What are the problems with these options, and what other alternatives might be suggested?

3. Toward the end of the article, the author suggests that well-meaning Christians might reach different conclusions on the question of sanctioning homosexual relationships based on the weight that they assign to three different factors. Identify your own position with regard to each of these:

4. To what extent does the lack of a life-partner deprive one of experiencing life in a way that God would call "good"?

5. To what extent does a homosexual relationship allow gays or lesbians to experience something similar to the intimacy of marriage that would usually be part of human experience?

6. To what extent can committed and monogamous relationships between homosexuals in our modern world be distinguished from the relationships that are denounced in the Bible?

For Further Reading

Brawley, Robert L., ed. *Biblical Ethics and Homosexuality: Listening to Scripture*. Louisville: Westminster John Knox, 1996.

Countryman, L. William. *Dirt, Greed, and Sex: Sexual Ethics in the New Testament and Their Implications for Today*. Minneapolis: Fortress Press, 1990.

Furnish, Victor Paul. *The Moral Teaching of Paul: Selected Issues*. 2d ed. Nashville: Abingdon, 1985.

Gagnon, Robert A. *The Bible and Homosexual Practice: Texts and Hermeneutics*. Nashville: Abingdon, 2001.

Hays, Richard B. *The Moral Vision of the New Testament: A Contemporary Introduction to New Testament Ethics*. San Francisco: HarperSanFrancisco, 1996.

Scroggs, Robin. *The New Testament and Homosexuality*. Philadelphia: Fortress, 1983.

Soards, Marion L. *Scripture and Homosexuality: Biblical Authority and the Church Today*. Louisville: Westminster John Knox, 1995.

2.

The Lutheran Reformation and Homosexual Practice

James Arne Nestingen

The original Lutheran documents concern two central themes—the justification of the godless and the vocations of everyday life. As Luther wrote in *The Freedom of the Christian*, when the death and resurrection of Christ Jesus restore us to the relationship for which we were created, setting us free from the powers of death and desolation, "the Christian is the perfectly free Lord of all, subject to none." At the same time, in Christ, the Christian is "the perfectly dutiful servant of all, subject to all," called into the service set out by the day.[1]

Convinced of the biblical priority of these themes for a church turned in on itself at the time of the Reformation, the original Lutherans did not attempt to build a completely new theological or ethical system. Instead, they took as their own the Catholic tradition of the church, attempting first to reorient its preaching and worship, and then to correct points where they thought it had gone astray. As they rethought the tradition, the Lutherans worked with distinctions they took to be required by their themes, such as the distinction between law and gospel, between the two kingdoms, and others.

Because they approached matters this way, there is no particularly Lutheran teaching on homosexual practice. Martin Luther, Philip Melanchthon, and others who wrote either unofficially or officially, clearly knew the standard biblical texts along with traditional Christian teachings. They were also well aware of violations, especially among an officially celibate clergy. While oftentimes critical of Roman Catholic views of sexuality, they accepted as a given, requiring little or no comment, the church's universal condemnation of homosexual practices. In fact, given their biblical way of thinking, the reformers might have wondered how the church's endorsement of homosexual practice ever became an issue for church-wide consideration.

This said, the Lutheran heritage still has something to say about approaching issues of sexual ethics. We may go about hearing its voice in two ways. One is to review the Lutheran sources and note the points that relate to sexual matters, using the classic distinctions to think them through. The second is to look at the contemporary interpretation of social ethics that has been authoritative for American Lutherans to see how it might apply.

Resources

Beginning with justification by faith puts a strong priority on the forgiveness of sins in its spoken and sacramental form. As a gathering of sinners assembled by the Holy Spirit for the preaching of God's Word and the administration of the sacraments, the church exists to assure those caught up under the powers of the world as we know it—be they personal, social, private, public, corporate, or cosmic forces—of the triune God's love in restoring the creation. The church is the church when it declares to sinners, sexual or otherwise, the promise of the gospel, and so serves their entering the relationships for which all were intended: faith, hope, and love. Since the Trinity is ultimately the speaker of this word, the one who authorizes its declaration, it is complete, unconditional, and free. The only possible parallels are creation out of nothing and the resurrection of the dead.

Distinguishing Law and Gospel

One of the first consequences of this priority involves the law. Thus, justification takes place "apart from the law," as the apostle Paul says, or "without the law" (Gal. 2:15-21). Or to put it in the language of the Gospel of John, since Christ is "the way, the truth and the life," the law cannot be (John 14:6; 1:17). But this raises an immediate question in the New Testament itself, in the Lutheran sources, and in alternative readings of the Christian faith: What about the law? There are moral requirements in Scripture, there are legal requirements in the state, and rules are everywhere! What are they for? Justification by faith requires a distinction between law and gospel, one of the key aspects of Lutheran thinking.

Luther answers the question as Paul did, correlating the law with sin. The gospel of God's love for sinners in Christ Jesus doesn't change—it is the first and last word. But when the gospel promise is spoken, declaring the forgiveness of sins, deliverance, and resurrection, the law appears in an entirely different light. It is reduced to its proper proportions, becoming a word as opposed to the Word.

Approached in this way, for the original Lutherans, the question of the law's purpose becomes a down-to-earth problem of description. What is the law for? The answer is not so much theological as it is a description of what the law actually does in human experience. While it can't engender love, hope, or faith, the law is generally good at keeping order. It is not perfect—not by any means—but in perhaps four out of five cases, the law brings enough restraint to keep things working as they are supposed to work. In this capacity, the law restrains evil and can also point to the need for justice and peace in the household, in the community, and in the larger world.

In the light of the gospel, another capacity of the law appears, one that appears in vague outlines apart from Christ Jesus. In the world as we now know it, the law has a way of turning against a person, focusing on the defining relationships to attack, to expose, or above all to accuse. The occasion of the law's attack might be a moral problem; more commonly, it has to do with a person's sense of standing in relation to the family, work, and the public, or to God. In fact, when the law assaults in this way, it shows its characteristic power in this life. It has a way of compounding itself in a person's sense of self until it becomes virtually demonic, an ally of sin and death. As it traditionally has been put, the law works wrath.

Distinguishing law and gospel in this way, Luther repeatedly preached and wrote on the Ten Commandments to show their place in the ordering of life. The Commandments are scriptural, they are fundamental to the law of Israel, and they have had an important place in the Catholic tradition. But to Luther their authority rests in the simple and direct way that they codify the fundamental relationships of everyday life. They formulate what is required of all people in the web of interdependence necessary to life.

Three commandments relate to sexual matters. In the traditional Catholic numbering, the Fourth says "Honor your father and mother." It is assumed here that life is inherently familial. Children enter the world out of a relationship between a woman and a man. By the act of parenthood, mother and father assume responsibility for the child—nurturing, protecting, and training until the child is mature enough to leave home. If the parents do not shoulder this responsibility, others will have to step in for the child. Delicate, complex, and basic to the shape of a child's life, family relationships by their very nature demand honor—a combination of love, deference, and respect flowing back and forth between parents and children. Though there are always exceptions, the early quality of family relationships generally plays itself out for a lifetime, for good or ill. As such, the commandment to honor is basic to the shape of life itself.

The Sixth Commandment follows suit. The prohibition of adultery rejects sexual relations, defined as mutual genital activity, apart from marriage. But as Luther interprets the commandment, the negative assumes the positive—that "husband and wife love and honor one another." Again, the nature of the relationship demands such a cherishing, not only because life begins sexually but also because intimacy thrives best where love and honor prevail. Uniting sinners for a lifetime carries high risk; the prohibition of adultery protects the whole family relationship so that its positive dimensions can develop.

Eliminating the original biblical commandment against graven images, the Catholic tradition split the biblical Tenth Commandment against covetousness into two, the Ninth dealing with the house, the Tenth with a person's relationships. Luther follows the tradition, explaining both commandments in terms of the craftiness, tricks, and enticements used by sinners to deprive others of what is rightfully theirs while still seeking to maintain a legal appearance.

While the numbering is the same, a difference between the Lutheran and the Catholic traditions shows up here. Following certain writings of Saint Augustine, who summed up the theology of the early church and laid the basis for medieval Catholicism, the church had focused on desire itself, and particularly sexual desire, to locate the prime sin. So in the Catholicism Luther and the reformers knew, the traditional language of sin, including words like "concupiscence" (insatiable desire), and "lust," was sexually charged. Inordinate desire breaks into disorder, turning people from the spiritual to the carnal, from the lofty concerns of the soul to the baser agendas of the flesh.

Luther and his colleague and friend Philip Melanchthon, the final editor of the Augsburg Confession and a major influence in the Lutheran Reformation, redefined the terms. As they saw it, the root or prime sin arises in the deeper regions of the human heart. The disordered loves of sexual longing grow out of the sinner's determination "to be wise, to know good from evil" (Gen. 3:5), and so to avoid death. They grow out of the desire to justify the self, to gain control of the sources of life and bend them to personal purpose, to become one's own project determining one's own significance and value. In the medieval Catholic tradition the Lutherans knew, the prime sin was sexual; as the Lutherans saw it, the prime sin was religious, seeking the power and value of life in "creatures, saints and devils," as Luther put it. Finally, it was idolatry—the sin of the First Commandment.

This difference between the medieval Catholic and Lutheran traditions plays itself out in relation to the Ninth and Tenth Commandments in general, and matters of sexuality in particular. Because the root sin is disordered sexual longing, the medieval church sought to regulate desire and restore order by setting up structures in which the truly devout withdrew from sexual contact. Monks and nuns had for centuries taken vows of celibacy; in the eleventh century, the same requirement was made of all the clergy. While marriage was honored as a sacrament, it was of a lesser order—the truly devout could be so only by renouncing sexual relations. Women in particular bore an onus, being held responsible for lust's continuing power.

The Lutherans went a different direction. Luther had had enough struggles with his own heart, and had spent enough time in the confessional listening to people's accounts of their personal battles, to know the limits of the law's power. It can regulate external behavior—such as the plots and schemes of the covetous—but the powers at work in the human heart are more controlling than simple willpower. Repressed desire multiplies against itself in sinners, gaining a life of its own and so even greater dominance. In the process, covetousness becomes idolatry, exalting the object of its longings—whether thing or person—beyond human proportions, possessing the desirer like grim fate. Even if the heart cannot be reached, the external act has to be restrained by law—for the sake of the one desiring, the safety of the desired, and the well-being of the community. Disordered sexual longings are not the prime sin, but sexuality is an aspect of life in which sin expresses its power and so demands regulation for everyone concerned.

At the same time, in proportion with all of the other aspects of human selfhood, sexuality is one of the great goods of creaturely life. With it, God gives the deep companionship of marital life. And through it, God continues to bestow life in the creation, using women and men as his "hands" or "channels" to create a future for the community and the earth itself. In this context, sexual desire reveals its goodness, bringing couples together to serve one another, God, and the community.

Recognizing both the limits of the law and the goodness of marital life, the original Lutherans were sharply critical of the medieval church's sexual regulations. "Experience has shown," they wrote, "how little it is possible to improve on nature." In the sixteenth century, the celibacy requirement was systematically broken, making hypocrites of those required to take the vows and leaving behind a long line of victims. Women caught up in such relationships were denied the protection of law; their children were stigmatized. As the Lutherans saw it, celibacy can be a gift of the Holy Spirit given for some extraordinary purpose; where that gift is not granted, even if the vows are externally kept, the power of creaturely longing expresses itself in other ways.

Two Kingdoms

Beginning with God's justifying work in Christ Jesus, Luther drew another distinction: that between two kingdoms or realms, two different ways in which God lays claim to creation and creature. One is the kingdom that comes in the preaching of Jesus, his death, and his resurrection—a decisive turn in the distribution of power in which God wrests back dominance from sin, death, and the devil. This kingdom extends from the present into the future. It comes now, "when God gives us his Holy Spirit so that we may believe his word and live godly lives," as Luther put it in the Small Catechism, and it will come "in heaven forever," when the forces of desolation are destroyed.

At the same time, God exerts his claim through another kingdom, composed of the various cultural assumptions, relationships, institutions, systems, and structures of this life. While these forms cannot bring in the new future, "the new age," as the New Testament calls it, they are a necessary part of life as we know it and accomplish all kinds of good. With other loosely associated forms of power and influence, they make up the earthly realm—the kingdom of this world. Through them, God works order, making the provisions necessary to approximate justice and peace.

Though Lutherans don't talk about it as commonly as Luther did, there is also a third, more elusive or shadowy kingdom in which the evil one and the forces of death seek to recover the control won by Christ Jesus in his death and resurrection. The devil seeks this goal by confusing the two kingdoms—by deluding us into thinking that God's rule frees Christians from the responsibilities of everyday life, for example, or by making human institutions ultimate. This third, shadowy kingdom gives itself away by its use of craft or deceit.

The two kingdoms also can be distinguished by the means God uses in them. God's rule in Christ comes through the gospel, whether in its preached or sacramental form. Through this word, the Holy Spirit creates faith, a free and merry confidence that fears, loves, and trusts God above all things, as Luther put it. All the other relationships and institutions in everyday life—the agencies of the earthly kingdom—depend upon the law and, in that context, accomplish their purposes. The family, the church as an organization, various levels of government, the economy, and the like are all maintained by cooperation, generally some degree of submission or obedience, just rewards or mutual respect and support.

The two-kingdom distinction sets a critical principle for believers to guard against the wily ways that can confuse them. When ultimate claims are made by human agencies—in the state, the church, or the family—they have to be brought back down to earth. At the same time, the two-kingdom distinction helps protect the goodness and integrity of creaturely relationships. Grasped by the Spirit in true faith, believers serve freely in both kingdoms, joyfully speaking the Word, delightfully loving the neighbor.

Describing how this works, the original Lutherans focused particularly on four relationships or callings, giving them close attention because they are life-creating or life-sustaining and so the decisive features of Christian service. The family forms and shapes our lives. Work, whether it grows out of family responsibilities or is pursued as gainful employment, is in all but the most unusual circumstances the means by which people become directly helpful in the community. The church, as well as a gathering around Word and Sacrament, is what has sometimes been called "an intermediate sociological structure"—an organization in which people meet and care for one another, serving the larger community and the world in life-giving ways. Citizenship—while it is commonly rough and ready, less intimate than the family, a looser bond than the church—unites people in the public services required for community life: schools, governance, the quest for justice and peace. There are many other relationships in which service is rendered, but these four are basic. In each of them God calls the faithful to the specific responsibilities of the love of the neighbor, among others.

This service to life rendered in the callings doesn't happen simply because of people's commitments. In fact, given the continuing force of the third kingdom, people suffer some of their deepest wounds in their families, are taken advantage of at work, vow never to go to another annual meeting of a congregation, and wonder if there is such a thing as good government. But in each of these relationships, and in all of the more specific vocations believers serve, God has set things up so that there is service, voluntary or involuntary. Even such a simple act as buying a quart of milk sends out ripples of benefit: to the farm family, the dairy, the store and its staff, the people who gather around the table to drink it. All vocations are turned toward service, with or without our aid.

So the vocations are the locations of Christian service. Sometimes it is free and joyful, believers going about their duties with virtually no awareness of the good resulting—giving themselves selflessly in their families, delighting in a job well done, contributing of themselves to the congregation, rejoicing in the privileges of citizenship. Sometimes the service is begrudged and hidden, God using a calling to wring some good out of a reluctant saint who will do only as much as absolutely has to be done. But God is at work, in Luther's language, using the creature as a hand or a channel through which goodness flows, or a "mask" behind which God can hide to continue caring for the creation.

Implications

Sorting through original Lutheran sources reinforces their coherence with the ecumenical consensus of the church in matters of sexual practice. Both Scripture and the church's tradition insist that God gave sexuality for marriage. Any form of mutual genital activity outside of marriage is prohibited. That said, however, there are some other clear implications in the sources.

First, when the justification of the godless is the first and last word, the center that holds Lutheran thinking together, the line dividing the unrighteous from the righteous, gets blurred. "Anything that does not proceed from faith is sin," Paul says (Rom. 14:23); in this life, as we know it, sin is not an occasional act but a condition in which everyone is implicated. That is as true for heterosexuals as for those who identify themselves as homosexuals. It is not a question of the really righteous versus the genuinely sinful. In a fallen world, sinners have to deal with other sinners. The absolution, the oral declaration of the forgiveness of sins, is God's word for all.

It is especially important to emphasize the forgiveness of sins in sexual matters. As many biblical stories indicate, sexuality has always been a difficult part of human relations, subject to all kinds of abuse. For countless people, women and men, sexual matters involve their deepest intimacies and wounds, ecstatic joys and profound disappointments. In virtually any conversation, there will be victims living in a hell of sorrow. If the word of forgiveness isn't given its proper place, the law will just take over, compounding itself to destroy.

Second, while the law can never be granted the last word, it still has *a* word about the shape of life. Because we are creatures who do not have life within ourselves as a possession but receive it from others, some relationships are normative: the relationship between wife and husband as well as between parents and children. By the goodness of God, life can and does continue even as these relationships are breached. But by the same token, because sexuality is so basic to these life-giving relationships, it can never be regarded as either a private right or a personal privilege. Heterosexual or homosexual, the sexual partner is always somebody's son or somebody's daughter, a brother or sister, who also stands under the obligation of law.

Because sexual relationships are so inherently public, the Commandments place desire under scrutiny. God uses it for good. Yet desire also can become profoundly destructive. For this reason, the experience of desire for mutual genital activity with another person or people cannot be regarded as an entitlement, as though a person has an inherent right to act it out. Neither does the persistence of such desire provide a positive basis of personal identity that entitles a person to special recognition by the community. In fact, for all the blessing that it can be, desire also contains a threat that has to be disciplined.

Third, marriage and the family are one of the defining callings, blessed by God. The words of Genesis, "Be fruitful and multiply, fill the earth and subdue it" (1:28), have a normative standing in the life of the church. Similarly, the God of Scripture has blessed marriage in a way that no other form of human companionship has been blessed. But neither the command to fruitfulness nor the blessing is particularly religious, mere ideas or concepts the original Lutherans picked out to impose on others. They have to do with the basic shape of life itself. From the beginning—however that beginning is conceived—women and men have united to create and care for their offspring, which has been the blessing of their union. The uniting may have been pleasant or hateful; the blessing may have been profoundly satisfying or had all the appearance of a curse; because of some other form of blessing or as a result of some evil, any number of people have perhaps not wanted to have anything to do with either the uniting or the offspring. But life cannot happen without some provision for and some protection of the relationship between the sexes.

Fourth, as an institution of the earthly kingdom, the church has both the right and the duty to set standards appropriate to itself. Gathering a membership, collecting offerings, occupying a space along a street or road, the church is a public institution. So, like other similar organizations, it establishes policies and expectations for its membership and its officers.

The Augsburg Confession defines two standards for the ministry. Article V describes ministry as an office established by the Holy Spirit for the preaching of the Word and the administration of the sacraments. In Article XIV, the authority of the office is limited by a proper call, which is the condition of a pastor's service.

American Lutherans have debated the interpretation of these articles. Some traditions have emphasized the word *office,* arguing that since God established the office, it has a prior authority of its own. Others have emphasized the word *call,* insisting that the authority of the ministry derives from the election of the congregation. In either case, whether handed down from above or granted from below, the authority of the ministry does not belong to the person who holds the office. Like anyone elected to a public office, a pastor leaves private life behind to exercise the authority necessary to carry out assigned responsibilities for the church. Nobody has a *right* to ministry. As an office of the church, it belongs to the church, a point to be emphasized as strongly as possible.

Historically there have been differences in the manner of electing pastors. Some Lutherans have wanted to give greater authority to the bishop who nominates candidates for call; others have wanted to protect the congregation's prerogatives. Either way, there is no proper call without the congregation's consent. So candidates are considered, preparation and experience are assessed, a vote is taken, and a call is issued. In its most common, printed form used among Lutherans, the call states various standards to which, as a condition of the office, the pastor agrees.

One of the standards is sexual. As preachers of the word and administrators of the sacrament, pastors commonly deal with people at times of deep vulnerability—in circumstances of birth and death, in situations of illness and personal need as well as celebration and thanksgiving. This gives pastors a peculiar combination of authority and intimacy so that people will speak with them as they do with no one else, whether family or friend. In such close relations, feelings that cross sexual lines may develop easily.

For this reason, the office of ministry by its very nature requires sexual reliability and accountability. A pastor who uses either the authority of the office or the intimacy that it creates to become involved in mutual genital activity with another person compromises herself or himself, the other person, and the office. In fact, in the experience of the church with such violations, the breach of office remains after the offending pastor leaves and will likely be detrimental for the next two or three pastors who are called to that congregation.

In the larger public life, the rough and ready common citizenship, a person's sexual behavior may be a matter of personal choice. But when a pastor accepts a call, the pastor's sexual behavior becomes a legitimate concern of the public institution that has elected to issue the call. In fact, where the church has neglected to maintain this standard, state legislatures and the courts have increasingly stepped in to enforce their own visions of sexual reliability. The state of Minnesota, for example, requires a background check of a pastor's sexual behavior over several years prior to call. When various state courts have ruled, they have commonly held synodical and national church bodies responsible for the sexual behavior of offending clergy, resulting in six-figure settlements. A society that routinely scrutinizes the sex life of its politicians can hardly be expected to discount such concerns for the clergy.

The same standards of sexual reliability that apply to heterosexual clergy come into play with the issue of the ordination of active homosexuals. In its current statement of *Vision and Expectations* for the clergy, the Evangelical Lutheran Church in America has made a distinction between orientation and practice—pastors claiming a homosexual orientation may be called to congregations provided that they remain celibate. Gay and lesbian clergy have challenged this policy, appealing to some of the original Lutheran sources to argue that celibacy is no more appropriate or realistic for them than it is for heterosexual clergy. In fact, homosexual advocates have argued that traditional Christian standards of fidelity cannot be applied to gays and lesbians because of differences in practice. Either way, given the church's standards and the holdings of state courts, all clergy are legally responsible for their sexual practices. If the church does change its policies on ordination, homosexual clergy will have to be willing to give a legally defensible account of their sexual practices. At the same time, the synods and the national church will have to be able to satisfy the courts that they have effectively monitored the sexual behavior of the clergy.

The Lutheran Social Ethic

Examining the Lutheran heritage, especially as it involves the gospel and the Commandments along with the most basic distinctions, provides orientation for discussing the issue of homosexual practice. But such a procedure also involves some risks. One is the reliability of the selection, given sinners' predilections for bias; another is changing times. The Lutheran reformers lived a long time ago; five hundred years makes a difference.

Generally, the church has taken on these problems through its teachers. Theologians have worked their way through the tradition, arguing the different ways in which the teachings of the Reformation apply today and debating one another's findings. A good example, generally considered reliable, is German theologian Helmut Thielicke's *The Ethics of Sex,* a separately published volume within a larger work.

As helpful as individual work might be, however, in dealing with a public issue, it is crucial to move beyond personalities and scholarly arguments to a corporate way of thinking that has been studied and refined over a period of time by people called together by the church for this purpose. In the heritage of the ELCA, one of the merging churches developed such a public way of applying the Lutheran heritage to current ethical problems. In fact, its value has been examined closely and recognized for its service to the larger church in such matters. This method has been summed up in the following three statements:

> First, that there is no sphere of life which is a law unto itself, autonomous of the absolute sovereignty of God, however free it must remain from ecclesiastical domination. Secondly, that all persons, apart from Christ, are capable of high degree of social justice in the building of a peaceful and humane society in which the Christian offers his or her critical co-operation and responsible participation. Thirdly, that it is in and through the personal and corporate witness of his faithful followers in their civic

vocations, as well as their church worship, that Christ's lordship—however hidden in its servant form—is made manifest in our communal life in contemporary society.[2]

Each of the statements in this summary of a contemporary Lutheran social ethic is helpful on the issue of homosexual behavior.

Individual and Community

First, one of the major differences between the time of the Lutheran Reformation and contemporary American public life is a change in the proportionate value of society and the individual. In the sixteenth century, life was inherently communal, one of the concerns of the reformers being to find a legitimate place for the individual. The founders of the American republic continued that quest in their own way, writing into the Declaration of Independence the conviction that, by nature, every person has a right to life, liberty, and the pursuit of happiness. The technological advances of the twentieth century turned the proportions. Whereas the reformers moved from the community to the individual, now the issue is moving from the individual to the public. In fact, given the rights of the individual, there is a common conviction that life is so inherently private that the community has no legitimate voice.

Recently, this way of thinking has also been applied to sexual matters. *Roe v. Wade*—the still controversial Supreme Court decision on abortion—established legal precedent for what many people now take as a given, arguing that sexuality is a personal matter, a right to be protected from communal regulation. The church has generally followed suit. So on numerous familial and sexual issues, Lutherans have either backed away from historical ethical standards—divorce regulations, for example—or simply remained silent. Thus, while parish pastors describe a social transformation in which most couples live together prior to marriage, the church has formally said little or nothing.

These cultural arguments are now being made on the issue of homosexual practice. Sexuality is a matter of personal preference, it is said, or a result of genetic and other forms of determination that take it beyond choice for the individual. Consequently, the church has no business continuing its opposition to gay and lesbian sexual expressions. Instead, it should bless committed homosexual relationships and ordain practicing homosexuals.

Cultures involve shared assumptions about the most basic relationships of life, sexual and otherwise. Such values are an essential part of the earthly realm; they are means through which God works for the sake of justice and peace, for the ordering of public life. For that reason, Lutherans have generally viewed cultural matters positively; by the same token, Lutherans have commonly, though not always, been very critical of the church's desire to dominate the culture. As Luther once said, "Better a wise Turk than a stupid Christian," that is, better to have in charge someone who really knows what is going on than to submit to pious pretense.

This acknowledged, however, the first statement in the above summary of a contemporary Lutheran social ethic points to a fundamental conflict. Though the culture may define sexuality as a personal right beyond the community's reach, Lutherans have historically insisted that "no sphere of life is a law unto itself, autonomous of the absolute sovereignty of God. . . ." There are two basic reasons for the church's continued disagreement with the culture in sexual matters.

To begin with, the deep change in public sexual mores in the United States has not and cannot eliminate the public dimension of sexuality. Birth control and the privatization of personal life have dramatically changed the way people think about sexual relations—it is no longer true that sexual intimacy necessarily involves the possibility of childbearing. By the very conditions of human life, however, the individual cannot be sexually autonomous but is of necessity part of the larger community: a family with its heritage, friends of the family, the community that supports it, the larger public. Withdrawal from such relationships doesn't nullify them—it just drives the connections underground, where, even if not immediately noticed, they exercise their influence. The web of human interdependence that shapes life makes sexual autonomy impossible. Accordingly, the community has not only the right but also the duty to set standards.

There is a strange contradiction at this point, the kind often found in the rough-and-tumble of cultural values. Many who have commonly argued for the dismissal of traditional sexual standards have, at the same time, strongly supported the closer regulation of the way people relate to one another in corporate life—in the workplace and in schools, for example—to protect against unwelcome sexual advances. One way or another, the community plays a part.

But for the church, there is another deeper level of concern. Life in Christ is at the same time, inextricably, life in community. The Holy Spirit, who calls through the gospel also and at the same time, gathers, to use the words of Luther's Small Catechism. As the apostle Paul writes in Romans 14:7-8, "We do not live to ourselves, and we do not die to ourselves. If we live, we live to the Lord, and if we die, we die to the Lord; so then, whether we live or whether we die, we are the Lord's." The risen Christ lays claim to us in all of our relationships, including the sexual. Under Christ's claim, in faith we are turned toward the neighbor in a love that "hopes all things, endures all things" (1 Cor. 13:7). The language of rights and the language of love are mutually exclusive—rights are established to preserve entitlements; love brings people together in mutual consideration.

But now this argument cuts both ways. On the one side, it stands against those who insist that the church adapt to cultural assumptions. In fact, the culture does have integrity of its own. Standards do vary in the different cultures of the world as people attempt to come to terms with the relationships that define them. There is something provisional about these standards—they can and should change, a fact that has to be respected. But the church has its own way of thinking, shaped around the death and resurrection of Jesus of Nazareth. In that logic, sexual self-assertion, the claim to entitlement, a demand for personal or communal submission, the multiplication of partners, the subordination of the other to self-fulfillment are all suspect on any terms. In fact, the desire to place the self beyond judgment—to become one's own creator, to gain control over creation, creature, and Creator for this purpose—is sin itself, no matter what the circumstance.

At the same time that it cuts against the assertion of autonomy, however, this way of thinking centers on God's call to the neighbor. If the languages of rights and love are mutually exclusive, love and dominance also are contraries. The Christ who lays claim to the bodies of the faithful is the one, now risen from the dead, who had a way of finding people who had been pushed to the margins. While none of these people in the Gospels is explicitly identified as gay or lesbian, they recur—the woman at the well, for example, or the woman taken in adultery—as those whose sexuality has become a crucifixion. If love is deaf to the language of power, it can certainly hear and recognize the calls of those who have been marginalized or abused.

This is a particularly important consideration with families. Citizenship, the church, and the family feature different kinds of relationships. So people don't expect the same of other citizens that they do of one another as church members; by the same token, as close as the Christian community becomes, it isn't as tight as a family and shouldn't be. Recognizing this, the church has to respect the advocacy of families supporting one of their own who has asserted a gay or lesbian identity. At the same time, families have to recognize that church relationships have an integrity of their own; while caring for its gay and lesbian members individually, the church as a community may have to set and maintain different policies for those who hold office within it.

Working Together for Good

"You meant it for evil," Joseph said to his brothers, who had cooked up a story to protect themselves after their father Jacob's death. "God used it for good" (Gen. 50:20). Because the forgiveness of sins blurs the line between insider and outsider, righteous and unrighteous, Lutherans have wanted, like Joseph, to emphasize the goodness God can accomplish through others, even if their intentions are questionable. So the second statement in the summary of contemporary Lutheran social ethics holds "that all persons, apart from Christ, are capable of high degree of social justice in the building of a peaceful and humane society in which the Christian offers his or her critical co-operation and responsible participation."

Considering a change in its policies, the church has first of all a responsibility to analyze accurately the standing of gays and lesbians in public life. As usual, this has a way of turning difficult, becoming much more complicated than advocates on either side of the issue want to allow. Both proponents and opponents of change have commonly generalized from anecdotes or stereotypes, using little or no evidence to support their claims.

An example of the difficulty, along with an illustration of the importance of factual data, appears in the statistics gathered by the Centers for Disease Control in Atlanta. The center reports three deaths of homosexuals in one year resulting from hate crimes. During the same year, seven thousand died as the result of unprotected sex between males. No doubt, each side has its own interpretation of the data, but the statistics do shed some light. Opponents of a changed policy will have to acknowledge the victims, even if they want to put the numbers in proportion. By the same token, while pointing out that AIDS is an equal opportunity killer, afflicting heterosexuals and homosexuals, proponents of changing the church's stand will have to acknowledge that the large number of deaths does indicate a problem.

Either way, because the church has a legal responsibility for its clergy, it cannot work on suppositions, projections, and possibilities—it has to recognize and address the evidence or face the public consequences. Dealing with the hard realities may not resolve the question. But it will put the church in a position to answer for itself.

At the same time, the summary of a contemporary Lutheran social ethic points out the importance of making positive assumptions about the opposition. Here again, there have been transgressors on both sides. On one, there is a long history of hateful, prejudicial treatment of gays and lesbians that has to be acknowledged and confessed. On the other, the appropriation of gospel language such as "Reconciled in Christ" for gay and lesbian advocacy implicitly places those who disagree on the outside.

Whatever stance is taken, in discussions among Lutherans, there is a basis for making positive assumptions about the other. God has shaped our vocations in such a way that all people contribute to the public good, in one way or another. And in fact, both those who support a change in the church's policies and those who oppose it have their contribution to make in public life, whether in the larger society or the church itself.

The Lordship of Christ Jesus

Finally, the summary of a contemporary Lutheran social ethic indicates "that it is in and through the personal and corporate witness of his faithful followers in their civic vocations, as well as their church worship, that Christ's lordship—however hidden in its servant form—is made manifest in our communal life in contemporary society."

As a political institution, a gathering of people assembled out of public life, the church shares characteristics with every other human enterprise. It applies standards and votes on policies; it accomplishes goals and also sometimes fails to meet its objectives; it is sometimes at peace and occasionally embroiled in conflict within itself. Compared with other voluntary institutions of public life, it is hard to see any noticeable difference between the church and the others.

But finally, even with its various divisions, the church is united around the conviction that there is another at work within it, the triune God, justifying the godless to restore both creature and creation to the relationships intended. For this purpose, God speaks a word of judgment on the sinners assembled. The Holy Spirit becomes the user of the law, calling into question the seemingly endless self-absorption of sinners who, turned in on themselves, seek to become a law unto themselves. But the word of judgment is preliminary to the last word, a word that is also ultimately the Holy Spirit's responsibility. It is the gospel, the word of pardon and release in Christ Jesus, the word of forgiveness and resurrection—finally, a word of freedom.

It is a different kind of freedom. The freedom rightfully celebrated in American public life is political—it is freedom of choice, the freedom of self-determination. The freedom of the gospel is freedom from choice, freedom to enter irretrievably into the defining relationships of everyday life in service to the neighbor. These relationships all involve a cross. To be part of a family, to go to work day after day, to be shaped by a congregation, to take up the duties of citizenship under the conditions of life as we know it, necessarily involves self-loss. But in these daily deaths, in this dying with Christ, there is also the hope of a resurrection like his. So in the hiddenness of the ordinary, in the encumbrances and contrariness of everyday responsibility, the good Lord takes hold of our bodies—hands, feet, and other members—to create the new future. Occasionally, in the deepest relationships of life, there are glimpses of what will be—in the tenderness that breaks through the hostilities that have divided people, for example, or in a quiet reassurance granted amid suffering. Such glimpses, however, move the faithful from the eye to the ear, to the word—whether in its preached or sacramental form—that bespeaks the new age dawning.

For all of its foibles, for all of its limitations, for all of its implications in the injustices of the world, the church is in the end a creature of God's word. It exists in, and can only continue in, this purpose. As Lutherans have heard it, this word realizes itself in a freedom that holds under the cross for the sake of the resurrection. That is a word for all, even if considerations of policy require placing limits on institutional endorsements and office holders.

Issues

Given these considerations of the Lutheran heritage, in its original form and as interpreted and applied more recently by Lutherans, three issues require examination as the church debates its policy of homosexual practice.

The first is ecumenical. Even after Luther's excommunication, the original Lutherans saw themselves as belonging within the Catholic tradition of the church. That tradition, which includes the vast majority of the world's Christians, continues to hold standards on homosexual practice that it understands to be required by Scripture and the faith itself. Though various individual interpreters have offered personal interpretations of the biblical passages involved, the church's ecumenical authorities have shown little willingness to change the historical standards or to regard them as a matter in which they are willing to accept difference. Debating its current policies, the ELCA will have to consider that endorsing practicing homosexuals by blessings or ordination would isolate it from the ecumenical consensus and alienate it from the very church bodies with which it has sought closer accords.

Second, while cultural standards on sexual matters have changed dramatically in recent decades, increasingly strict legal provisions regulate the sexual behavior of clergy. Under this rule of law, gays and lesbians seeking to practice their homosexuality while serving as clergy must be willing to provide a public accounting of their sexual relationships. The church, both synodically and nationally, will have to decide whether it is willing to assume with homosexuals the legal and financial responsibility that the law has already imposed on it for monitoring the sexual practices of heterosexual clergy.

Third, in the issues of blessing gay and lesbian unions and ordaining practicing homosexuals, there is a fundamental conflict between cultural and traditional Christian views of sexuality. Contemporary culture has privatized sexual relationships, regarding them as a matter of personal desire and therefore of right and entitlement. Lutherans, in the context of the larger Catholic tradition, have regarded sexuality as inextricably tied to the vocation of the family, as a matter of honoring and cherishing the other and the community.

In, with, and under these three issues, intertwined among them, another matter shows through—the defining issue for Lutherans. Using another person for sexual self-gratification, with or without consent, reduces the other to an object or an occasion—a serious enough problem by itself, no matter how or where it happens. But in the original Lutheran ways of thinking, the fundamental point is always justification by faith. Seeking life in "creatures, saints and devils"—trying to find the significance or value of one's self in personal terms, attempting to establish an identity beyond God's judgment, is idolatry. In an older language, it is "justification by works," whether the doings are religious or apparently irreligious, pious or profligate.

The church exists for one purpose, to declare Holy Absolution, to speak Christ's forgiving word, to proclaim the justification of the godless in its preached and sacramental forms. There has always been a special dimension to this promise for those who have been caught up in their own sexuality. So the ELCA has committed itself to a special welcome for gays and lesbians. But just for that reason, just because of the justification wrought in Christ Jesus, the church has to challenge all of the other justification schemes that are offered. Having examined the Lutheran heritage, in its early writings and its authoritative interpretation, it is impossible to avoid the conclusion drawn by Wolfhart Pannenberg from the biblical evidence. A leading ecumenical theologian, he holds that a church that rejects the traditional teaching on homosexual practice can be neither evangelical nor Lutheran, no matter what it calls itself.[3]

Discussion Questions

1. Do you agree that affirming homosexuality and blessing its unions amounts to a form of self-justification apart from justification in Christ by grace through faith? Does this make the prospect of changing the church's policy regarding the recognition of gay and lesbian persons a church dividing issue?
2. Given the strong biblically based emphasis on marriage and family in the Lutheran tradition, is it conceivable that same-sex unions could share a similar vocation?
3. What are some of the most important contributions we can make from our theological and ethical heritage as we encounter the attitudes toward sexuality in our contemporary culture?
4. How much influence should the views of other Christian denominations have in Lutheran deliberations on matters of homosexuality?

For Further Reading

Bornkamm, Heinrich. *Luther on the Old Testament.* Translated by Eric and Ruth Gritsch. Edited by Victor I. Gruhn. Philadelphia: Fortress Press, 1969.

Lazareth, William H. *Christians in Society: Luther, the Bible and Social Ethics.* Minneapolis: Fortress Press, 2001.

Luther, Martin. "The Small Catechism" and "The Large Catechism," in Robert Kolb and Timothy R. Wengert, eds., *The Book of Concord.* Minneapolis: Fortress Press, 2000.

Thielicke, Helmut. *The Ethics of Sex.* New York: Harper and Row, 1964.

Wingren, Gustaf. *Luther on Vocation.* Translated by Carl C. Rasmussen. Philadelphia: Muhlenberg Press, 1957.

Notes

1. Martin Luther, "The Freedom of the Christian," in Jaroslav Pelikan and Helmut Lehmann, eds., *Luther's Works,* American Edition (Philadelphia and St. Louis: Muhlenberg Press and Concordia Publishing House), 31, 257ff..

2. William H. Lazareth, "Christian Faith and Culture," in Harold C. Letts, ed., *Christian Social Responsibility* (Philadelphia: Muhlenberg Press, 1957), 3, 74. See also William H. Lazareth, *Christians in Society: Luther, the Bible and Social Ethics* (Minneapolis: Fortress Press, 2001), 29. For an evaluation of the standing of this social ethics in Lutheranism, see Robert Benne, *The Paradoxical Vision: A Public Theology for the Twenty-first Century* (Minneapolis: Fortress Press, 1995), 120; and Christa R. Klein and Christian D. von Dehsen, *Politics and Policy: The Genesis and Theology of Social Statements in the Lutheran Church in America* (Minneapolis: Fortress Press, 1989), 179–290. Benne, along with Klein and von Dehsen, are quoted in Lazareth's more recent study, 29.

3. Wolfhart Pannenberg, "You Shall Not Lie with a Male: Standards for Churchly Decision-Making on Homosexuality," trans. Leonard R. Klein and Christian D. von Dehsen, Lutheran *Forum* 30, no. 1 (February 1996): 28–29.

3.

Rethinking Christian Sexuality: Baptized into the Body of Christ

Martha Ellen Stortz

Introduction: Beginning with Baptism

Sex used to be a topic avoided in polite company. Now everyone is talking about it. The conversations are impassioned and rarely polite. Skirmishes in the sexuality wars leave people angry and polarized. Lutherans wonder: Will our conversations be any different?

I argue that these conversations on sexuality will be different if Christians begin with their primary identity. Christians find that primary identity in baptism, not in sexual orientation. In addition, baptism gives Christians a common orientation and charts a common behavior on issues of sexuality. Christian conversations on sexuality ought to begin with baptismal identity, orientation, and behavior. Beginning with baptism promises to keep conversations polite; it will also keep them faithful.

Social critic Andrea Dworkin speaks to the importance of identity. Dworkin observes that historically people have been killed for their gender, race, color, or ethnicity, and she speaks of the "first identity" or "identity of primary emergency" as that for which a person might have to face death.[1] A Jewish woman in Nazi Germany might be disprivileged as a woman, but she would be sought out and slaughtered as a Jew. Being a Jew, then, would be her first identity, the "identity of primary emergency."

For Christians the "identity of primary emergency" is being a Christian. Indeed, Christians might be a far more endangered species than they care to believe. Christians receive their primary identity through baptism. Baptismal identity organizes all other facets of their public and private lives. Baptism places Christians in a community of others who have been similarly marked. It incorporates them into the body of Christ.[2] Indeed, baptism makes Christ's body the primary body of reference in sexual relationships.

Two decades ago, a young lesbian Christian testified before a church task force on homosexuality: "It's not just another issue that the church is studying;

59

it's my life." Her plea reminds Christians that their discussions on sexuality touch some people more directly than others. Her plea also raises the question of where people place their primary identity. For example, I would classify myself as a "feminist Christian" rather than a "Christian feminist." My primary identity is being a Christian; being a feminist follows. I wonder how the young woman above would identify herself: as a "lesbian Christian" or a "Christian lesbian." The argument presented here invites all Christians, whether homosexual or heterosexual, whether married, partnered, or single, to find their primary identity in baptism. What would Christian moral deliberation look like if it began with baptism?

Moral Deliberation: Considering Four Sources

Moral deliberation does not begin in a vacuum. Four sources shape Christian moral deliberation: Scripture, tradition, reason, and experience. The task of a community of faith is to evaluate evidence from each of these sources and to provide its congregations with guidance.

With chapters on the Lutheran tradition, the biblical witness, scientific reason, and the experience of minority communities, this volume lays the groundwork for the task of moral deliberation. Scholars alone cannot resolve the issues. Moral deliberation is a process of prayerful discernment in community. Considering accounts from Scripture, tradition, reason, and experience is only the beginning of deliberation. Deliberation becomes incarnate as Christian communities read and speak, listen and pray. The apostle Paul reminded the churches: "For now we see in a mirror, dimly, but then we will see face to face. Now I know only in part; then I will know fully, even as I have been fully known" (1 Cor. 13:12). At times Christians feel like spelunkers exploring a huge cavern armed with only a few candles. They can see only what their feeble lights illumine: the space before them. They can only guess at the dimensions of the entire cavern, but they can speak with modesty and conviction about what is in front of them.

As Christians think and pray together, let us be guided by words the disciples offered in the midst of another debate that almost divided the early Christian church. Like our debate over sexuality, their struggle concerned the question of belonging. Would Gentile Christians be subject to the same purity codes, including circumcision and food laws, as their Jewish Christian brothers and sisters? People were ready to leave the church over this issue. The disciples listened, prayed, and deliberated. They could never know fully the consequences of their actions, but they finally spoke to what was in front of them. "For it has seemed good to the Holy Spirit and to us . . ."(Acts 15:28). With all due modesty and conviction, let us follow their lead.

Scripture: "One Flesh" in Christ

When they face the task of moral deliberation, Christians first turn to Scripture. What does the Bible say? The move is instinctive, but the answers are not always clear. As Mark Allan Powell has shown in his contribution to this volume, using Scripture in moral deliberation demands a complex conversation. The biblical text and its world must be allowed to speak to the contemporary world. Christians must allow the biblical witness to challenge them, not simply echo what they want to hear.

The conversation requires listening to the biblical world as well as to our own. Many contemporary moral issues do not surface for the biblical authors, nor do we address these issues in ways the authors would have understood. For example, the Bible has nothing to say about ordaining homosexuals or blessing their relationships. Scripture condemns homosexual behavior but remains unaware of homosexual orientation. Moreover, the biblical texts refer almost exclusively to relations between men; only Romans 1:26 treats women. How should we use Scripture in moral deliberation on sexuality?

These ancient texts make a claim on Christians. They praise the God whom we worship, and they present the experience of believers upon whose shoulders we stand. Scripture makes a moral claim on us in two ways. First, it tells us who we are. More specifically, Scripture tells us *whose* we are. If we turn to the Bible only for advice on the conduct of our own lives, we miss the story the Bible narrates about the ways and workings of God. The Father's mystery of creation; the life, death, and resurrection of Jesus; the Spirit who moves over the face of creation: Scripture tells us who God is. As creatures of this kind of God, we live inside the life of the Trinity. Who we are depends on *whose* we are.

Second, Scripture guides us in what to do and what not to do. Sometimes its counsel occurs in clear and specific commandments: "You shall not bear false witness against your neighbor" (Exod. 20:16). At other times, scriptural advice is lodged in more general principles that the listener must apply to his or her own concrete circumstances: "What does the LORD require of you but to do justice, and to love kindness, and to walk humbly with your God?" (Mic. 6:8). Sometimes biblical counsel requires that we examine the contours of a parable and shape our own lives accordingly. Parables do not yield specific guidelines for behavior; they invite analogical reflection instead. The parable of the prodigal son does not leave its readers with a rule but rather invites them to play the role of three complex characters: a wasteful young man, his envious but upright older brother, and a father who forgives the excesses in both of his sons. As readers probe the parable's three central figures, they discover patterns of feeling and acting that interpret their own experience. Parables too contain counsel for the moral life.

Biblical counsel requires translation. The texts speak in a specific context. The words often do not translate easily into our own situation. For example, the story of Sodom and Gomorrah (Gen. 19) features prominently in contemporary discussions of homosexuality, and the "sin of Sodom" has long been understood as homosexuality. However, as biblical scholars and historians explored the texts and contexts of these two cities, they reported that the "sin of Sodom" was gross inhospitality and sexual violation. The men of the city plotted a sexual attack upon male strangers who were guests in Lot's household. The incident destabilizes modern categories of homosexual and heterosexual. Many of the men who sought to violate Lot's visitors may have had wives at home. These Sodomites wanted to protect their turf, and they resorted to a practice of sexual violence commonplace in the ancient world: rape of prisoners or strangers, regardless of gender. An understanding of the text of Genesis 19 demands an understanding of the context in which it was written.

Pointing to the unique context of Genesis 19, many dismiss the text's claim on us. After all, they argue, it is not really about homosexuality as we know it. I disagree. The text claims us, because we are people who worship the same God the book of Genesis reveals. Genesis 19 challenges us by addressing the violence of many debates about homosexuality. Too many of these impolite conversations display the "sin of Sodom" in the lack of civility one side shows the other. Whether the charge is "homophobe" or "politically correct left-wing liberal," the text reveals the sin in such name-calling to be inhospitality. More sharply, Genesis 19 demands that we acknowledge the violence in this kind of profiling. The text exhorts people of God to be generous to one another, if they claim to belong to a God who embodies generosity.

I propose a more generous reading of Scripture. Typically, when people ask what the Bible says about homosexuality, they want advice on what to do. They look for guidance encapsulated in clear and specific statements on a particular topic, often ignoring the more complex moral guidance contained in Scripture. What if Christians also looked to Scripture for insight into identity? What if they probed the whole issue of *whose* they were? What if Christians asked about baptism?

The apostle Paul finds baptism an important beginning point for his own discussions of sexuality. Speaking to vastly different communities in Rome, Ephesus, and Corinth, Paul focuses on baptism as a way of discussing Christian identity, orientation, and behavior. His counsel does not always tell people what to do. Rather, Paul elaborates on what God has done for them in Christ Jesus. Paul frames Christian identity as a matter of belonging: "You belong to Christ, and Christ belongs to God" (1 Cor. 3:23). Identity is a matter of belonging. Who they are depends on *whose* they are.

Baptism joins Christians into the body of Christ. As incorporation into the body, the rite of baptism has a double character. It is at once a rite of initiation and a rite of penance. As a rite of initiation, baptism forms Christian community. Baptism confers a name, but Christians should be clear about the name conferred. Too often baptism is reduced to mere christening. It becomes reduced to the ceremony in which an infant receives his or her given name, "Mary Elizabeth Wolff" or "Christian Alexander Bauer."

In fact, baptism confers a different name, "child of God," and that name signals membership in a dangerous community. As children of God we are incorporated into the body of another of God's children, Jesus Christ, the Son of God. When Christians think about sexuality, Christ's is the body they ought to think about first.

Baptism is also a rite of penance. As members of Christ's body, we are incorporated into Christ's death. The apostle Paul writes to the Romans: "Do you not know that all of us who have been baptized into Christ Jesus, baptized into his death?" (Rom. 6:3). All that threatens to displace our primary identity as members of the body of Christ must be put to death. Identification with a nation, an ethnic group, a career, a family, an orientation: all that vies for primary identity within the Christian must die to allow for resurrection in Christ, the ultimate loyalty. The apostle continues, "Just as Christ was raised from the dead by the glory of the Father, so we too might walk in newness of life"(6:4). In the new life these attachments will be ordered and reoriented to Christ.

In the double movement of penance and initiation, baptism redefines identity. Gone are the old gods; in their place is membership in the body of Christ. In defining their primary identity in terms of baptism, Christians shift their primary loyalties out of the realm of biological family and into the realm of Christian community. Accordingly, sexuality moves from the private sphere into the public sphere. With baptism we acknowledge that who we are body, mind, soul, and spirit is a public matter. With incorporation into the body of Christ, we confess that what we do in our bodies impacts the body of Christ.

The apostle Paul underscores this reality in writing to the pleasure-loving Corinthians. They frequented prostitutes, both male and female. The sexuality wars sent biblical scholars back to texts like 1 Corinthians 6:9-10 to figure out what Paul might have meant by "fornicators, idolaters, adulterers, male prostitutes, and sodomites." These forays are helpful, but finally beside the point. Paul is not so worried about the gender of the prostitute's body; he is more worried about the welfare of the body of Christ. Paul appeals to baptism in addressing the Corinthians' sexual practices:

> Do you not know that your bodies are members of Christ? Should I therefore take the members of Christ and make them members of a prostitute? Never! Do you not know that whoever is united to a prostitute becomes one body with her? For it is said, "The two shall be one flesh." But anyone united to the Lord becomes one spirit with him (1 Cor. 6:15-17).

What our culture considers a private matter, Paul regards as an important concern of the community. Paul intensifies his rhetoric several verses later, when he repeats to the community of Christians: "Your body is a temple of the Holy Spirit within you"(1 Cor. 6:19). The Greek words for "your" and "you" are plural, indicating that Paul speaks to many. These bodies become one "body," the body of Christ. This body is a temple for the Christ's spirit. As far as Paul is concerned, what Christians do with their bodies affects not only one another but also the body of Christ in which they dwell (1 Cor. 6:19). What a Christian does with his body matters on several levels: it affects him; it affects others; it affects the body of Christ.

Indeed, Paul takes incorporation into the body of Christ so seriously that he takes a text traditionally applied to marriage, "The two shall be one flesh" (Gen. 2:24), to describe the relationship between Christ and the church. Again, Paul turns to talk of "one flesh" when speaking to the Christians at Ephesus. "'For this reason a man will leave his father and mother and be joined to his wife, and the two will become one flesh.' This is a great mystery, and I am applying it to Christ and the church" (Eph. 5:31-32).

This passage from Genesis has been much cited in the sexuality wars, as scholars debate whether the union of "one flesh" ought to refer exclusively to male-female relationships or whether it might be extended to female-female or male-male relationships. Reading the text in his own context and unaware of contemporary debates, Paul moves "one flesh" out of the realm of human sexuality entirely. He applies the union to Christ and the church: Christ and the church are "one flesh." A Christian enters the church through the rite of baptism.

Scripture informs Christians as they deliberate on matters of sexuality. Biblical scholars and theologians have written much about texts that directly and indirectly address issues of homosexuality. Are these the only scriptural texts that Christians should consider? Perhaps we would be instructed by Paul's example of framing sexuality in terms of baptism. Writing to three communities as different as congregations in San Francisco, California; St. Cloud, Minnesota; and Columbia, South Carolina, Paul counsels Christians to remember their baptism. Here they would find their primary identity, their primary orientation, and counsel for behavior.

Tradition: Learning from Luther

Tradition provides another resource for moral deliberation. The witness of Christians from the past offers both a window to and a mirror on the present. Contemporary Christians look through a window onto centuries and cultures much different from their own. Yet every window also acts as a mirror, reflecting back an image of the ones looking. As we look into the past, we find things that strike us as odd or simply laughable. Those moments tell us most about ourselves and what we take for granted. We are gently reminded that things were not always as they are in our times. If we take tradition seriously, then, Christians stand to learn as much about the present as the past.

Looming large in the tradition to which Lutherans appeal is the figure of Martin Luther himself. On issues of sexuality, Luther faced his own task of moral deliberation. Marriage was an institution as much in crisis as the church, and Luther sought reform on both fronts. James Nestingen masterfully summarizes Luther's proposals for both. Here I focus on Luther's own task of moral deliberation. As he deliberated, Luther considered witness from the same four sources Christians consult today: Scripture, tradition, reason, and experience.

Luther found his own experience deeply contradictory. On one hand, marriage in the Roman Church was regarded as a sacrament and subject to clerical control, which meant long lists of rules and restrictions regarding union. On the other, celibacy was clearly the higher calling, required of priests, monks, and nuns. As Luther looked around him, he saw a host of good priests who had not been able to be celibate but lived in shame with a woman and a house full of children. These priests were doing good ministry, and Luther argued that they were "married in the sight of God." Why could they not be married in the eyes of the church?

Luther's own experience grounded his approach to sexuality, and he regarded sexuality with an earthy realism and a great deal of humor. For celibacy was the "gift," but clearly one that was rarely given. Celibacy should not be required of ordained priests. Writing to the German princes, Luther lamented the Roman practice of enforced celibacy: "The pope has as little power to command this as he has to forbid eating, drinking, the natural movement of the bowels, or growing fat."[3] Sexuality for Luther was basically a part of being human, blessed with the delicious ambiguity of all creation.

This ambiguity was something of which Luther was well aware. On specific matters Luther acted with a compassionate pastoral realism. If they did not manifest the gift of celibacy, priests should be allowed to marry, and Luther restructured congregations to support their families financially. Luther saw sexuality as a basic human need, and he identified marriage as the arena in which it could be justly and joyously exercised.

Human marriages should be patterned on the "true marriage" between Christ and the believer. Looking to Scripture for counsel, Luther turned to Paul in his letter to the Ephesians. It was the passage discussed above, in which Paul puzzles over the "one flesh" union referred to in Genesis 2:24. Where Paul applied the "one flesh" union to Christ and the church, Luther applied it to the union between Christ and the individual believer, intensifying Paul's rhetoric. Faith unites the soul to Christ, "as a bride is united with her bridegroom." Luther continued:

By this mystery, as the Apostle teaches, Christ and the soul become one flesh. And if they are one flesh and there is between them a true marriage—indeed the most perfect of all marriages, since human marriages are but poor examples of this one true marriage—it follows that everything they have they hold in common, the good as well as the evil.[4]

Through this "most perfect of all marriages," Christ and the believer share all things in common. Christ takes on the sins of the believer, and the believer in turn takes on the goodness of Christ. Luther described this union in words from that most erotic of biblical books, the Song of Solomon: "My beloved is mine and I am his" (Song of Sol. 2:16).

In this description of the relationship between Christ and the believer, the familiar language of justification gives way to a metaphor of sexual union. Luther's description of the union between Christ and the believer comes more from the wedding chamber than the courtroom. The sacraments of baptism and the Lord's Supper sustained this relationship. In baptism Christians are taken into Christ's body; in the Lord's Supper they take Christ's body into their own as food and drink. Put in such terms, it is easy to see why Luther found sexuality an appropriate and powerful metaphor to describe the life of faith. Bodies matter, and Christ's body matters most!

Baptism incorporates Christians into the body of Christ. Because they become part of Christ's body, the bodies of believers matter too. As he discussed baptism, Luther stressed its physical character. Baptism extends a physical sign of God's grace to the physical manifestation of human nature: bodies. Water is crucial: it renders the sacrament "external so that it may be perceived and grasped by the senses and thus brought into the heart" ("Baptism," the Large Catechism). Through the washing of bodies and water, God's grace enters the heart. Baptism allows the body to mentor the soul.

Baptism is both a one-time event and a lifelong process. Living out one's baptism takes a lifetime. For this reason Luther encouraged a "daily return" to baptism. The Christian might choreograph that daily return in various ways: a bowl of water on the dining room table, a prayer as she washes her face each morning, a hearty "Amen" in the shower, a petition in family prayer. The daily return to baptism reminds Christians that, as members of Christ's body, they belong to Christ. This sense of belonging, described by Luther as the "most perfect marriage," shapes every other relationship, particularly our earthly marriages and partnerships.

Reason: What Can We Know about Being Human?

Reason counts as another source of Christian moral deliberation, but what counts as "reason"? Luther himself often referred to it as a "whore," indicating his distaste for the highly rationalistic scholastic theology in which he had been trained. Under duress, however, Luther offered highly rational defenses of his positions. When they consult reason as a source in contemporary moral deliberation, contemporary Christians consider normative accounts of the human person from outside the discipline of theology: e.g., from the biological and social sciences, moral philosophy, philosophical ethics, anthropology, and cross-cultural studies.

Sexuality studies to date have depended heavily on the biological and psychological sciences in an effort to understand whether or not homosexuality is a choice. Some argue that sexual preference *is* a choice, and homosexuals should choose heterosexuality through counseling, prayer, and intensive therapy. Others argue that sexual preference is biologically or developmentally determined, and homosexuals should be allowed the exercise of their sexuality. In addition, churches should adapt by welcoming them and blessing their unions.

When predecessor church statements addressed the topic of homosexuality in 1970 (Lutheran Church in America) and 1980 (American Lutheran Church), they pointed to the "inconclusive" nature of scientific evidence. Some three decades later, scientific evidence proves only more confusing. In his chapter in this volume, Daniel Olson surveys the current state of the scientific explanations for homosexuality. Scientific studies suggest factors that include genetic determination, maternal hormonal level during pregnancy, birth order, parental behavior during infancy, and cultural pressures. As an aid to the debate on homosexuality, Olson himself finds the scientific studies of anger more helpful to Christian conversation than scientific studies on sexuality.

Evidence from the biological and psychological sciences must be considered carefully as Christians engage in moral deliberation. But have we given scientific testimony too much weight? Scientific terminology directs Christian thinking on sexuality. Categories such as homosexuality and heterosexuality, orientation and behavior, practicing and nonpracticing, direct the debate. How helpful are these binary oppositions for Christian discussion? I remember talking to a gay man about being a "practicing homosexual." "Practicing?" he said. "I think I got it right the first time." We laughed at the time, but the man died of AIDS several years later, still a faithful member of a church that could not find a language to help him reflect on the sexual practice appropriate to being part of the body of Christ.

Does science provide the only rational account of human flourishing that Christians should consider? Letting the biological and psychological sciences serve as the sole source of reason in moral deliberation may leave us with too shallow a pool of information on the human person.

I propose consulting another source of knowledge: moral philosophy, particularly its accounts of the human need to make and keep promises. Philosopher Hannah Arendt signals the importance of promise-making in her masterful book *The Human Condition.*[5] Arendt ranked as a philosopher, but she saw her task more concretely. She aimed to help people "think what we are doing" in the most basic activities of life: work, speech, and action.

Arendt explores a reflexive relationship between promise-making and community. Promises create community; community enables promises to be made and kept. Promise-making creates and sustains human community. Arendt fears that, because of the darkness of the human heart, people find it difficult to "guarantee today who they will be tomorrow." Promise-making guards against basic human unpredictability. Professions like ministry or law or medicine function in a web of promises. Some of these are explicit, like the vows made in an ordination service; others are implicit, like the expectations of professional competence that one brings to a consultation with a lawyer. A doctor tells a patient: "Take two aspirin and call me in the morning." The advice works because the patient knows her doctor will be there in the morning.

A community both enables and requires people to make promises. On one hand, the community expects fidelity from its members; on the other, the community supports people in keeping their promises. A tired physician drags herself to the office, only to be refreshed by the work to which she has committed herself. A pastor dreads a prickly discussion about the new building project. To his surprise, he finds he has led the discussion to a compromise everyone can affirm. Communities often help people become better at what they have pledged to be.

We do not have to read the whole of Arendt's *The Human Condition* to find out about promise-making. Christians know about promise-making in their bones, because promise-making and promise-keeping are central to Christian practice, if we could just "think what we are doing." Two examples help us access what we already deeply know: the practices of baptism and marriage. These core practices ratify a general human need to make and keep promises; they illustrate the reflexive relationship between promises and community.

Baptism: Promises for Life

Lutherans favor infant baptism, and the practice highlights the importance of promise-making. After all, an infant is too young to choose baptism. The community chooses on his or her behalf and supports that choice with a chorus of promises. The community acts on behalf of the infant, making promises he or she cannot yet understand, speaking words he or she will need a lifetime to comprehend, vowing support for as long as the child shall live. Doubtless not all in the community making these bold promises will even be around to celebrate the child's sixteenth birthday. No matter. Others will pick up the task. Soon the infant will mature to adulthood and bring his or her own children to the community for baptism, adding his or her own promises to the chorus of others.

The baptismal liturgy welcomes new members in a symphony of promises. There are promises to renounce the devil, to embrace the Trinity, to teach a new Christian the faith. There are no spectators in a baptismal liturgy. Everyone participates. Promises bind the community and God, the infant to God, the infant and the community, the members of the congregation themselves. Promises create and sustain this community in the body of Christ. That body exists as a community of Word and Sacrament to support the promises it makes.

Marriage: A Safeguard against Irreconcilable Difference

Similarly, marriage ceremonies feature a network of promises: between two people, between the couple and God, between the couple and a community, between a community and God. Two people promise to be faithful to one another. This promise involves sexual exclusivity and emotional fidelity; it binds them together for life. They make this promise before God, and in so doing pledge to keep God at the center of their relationship.

The couple also makes its promise in community. Two people enter the community as a couple and pledge themselves to the common good. The community may hold them accountable to the promises they have made. But the community also reciprocates with promises of its own, pledging accountability to the couple in its midst. Any union between two people faces irreconcilable differences and needs a community that can help people stay together in good times and in bad.

The two examples come from an ecclesiastical framework, but they reveal a basic human need to make and keep promises. As Arendt notes, promises guard against unpredictability, and humans flourish only if they can rely on themselves and others. Children need to know that the parents who tuck them in at night will be there the next morning and the next morning and the next. In a way, their children's need engenders in parents the desire to be the best parents they can be. By living out promises people become the kind of people they have pledged to be.

At this writing the Roman Catholic Church wrestles with the sexual misconduct of its priests. Survivors break their silence with stories of physical abuse they suffered as children. They trace the fault lines of abuse into their adult lives: fear, emotional uncertainty, spiritual distress. It is the wreckage of broken promises. Humans are, as the psalmist offered, "fearfully and wonderfully made," a unity of body, mind, soul, and spirit (Ps. 139:14). Promises kept preserve that unity, and promises broken shatter it.

Experience: Wise As Serpents, Innocent As Doves

Experience is the most difficult source to consider, partly because on this subject everyone is an expert. Experience often gets presented as innocent and uncut, but in fact it never comes without editing. Once something gets packaged and labeled as "experience," other hands have shaped it. Language and culture are among the hands that shape experience. Each has had important impact on the sexuality wars.

What Language Shall We Offer?

Christians could not share their stories without language; nor without language could they grasp the stories that shape them all: the story of Jesus and the kingdom of God, the story of exodus and promised land, the story of an ark, a flood, a rainbow, and a promise. These are stories that shape us. As we tell and retell them, we shape them.

These are not the only stories that shape us. There are stories of family and nation, stories of a profession or interest group, stories of a racial/ethnic group, outsider or insider stories. These stories also shape people, and as Christians move through the world, they become multilingual, able to speak in many different languages and adept at knowing what language to use in which context.

What language have Christians offered in the sexuality wars? In their past statements on sexuality, Lutherans have joined other mainline Protestant denominations in speaking of sexuality as a "gift" of God given to all people. Clearly Christians do not wish to sound prudish in a culture that worships sexuality, but it may be worth considering whether such language expresses the depth of Christian convictions about the human person, saved and sinning. Lutherans in particular speak with insight and realism of persons as *simul justus et peccator,* both saved and sinful. Yet when speaking of sexuality in recent studies, Lutherans present sexuality as "gift," suggesting that it is the one facet of human nature that is all *justus* and no *peccator,* all saved and not sinful. This makes it difficult to speak of the many and various ways in which sexuality itself is in need of redemption, like the rest of human nature. It is not the task of this article to present a taxonomy of carnal sin, but I would say only that the list is long and inclusive of both genders and all orientations. Moreover, "gift-language" leads all too easily to regarding sexuality as an entitlement or a right, which James Nestingen's chapter for this volume rightly challenges as inappropriate to Christian discipleship. Rather, Christians should view the whole of life as gift, one bestowed for worship of God and service to neighbor.

When gift-language is restricted to sexuality, it puts Christians in a bind. It leaves them unable to specify that sexuality is a gift to *the community,* not simply a gift to the individual. Baptized bodies are a matter of public concern. Further, gift-language risks elevating and idealizing sexuality. Faithful Christians wind up wondering if they are getting enough of the gift, opening it in the right way, or simply weird if they find themselves interested in other things. Finally, gift-language makes it difficult for Christians to acknowledge the destructive capacities of sexuality, e.g., narcissism, rape, domestic violence, child abuse and pedophilia, and abusive and exploitative sexual practices.

Where is Luther's earthy realism concerning sexuality, something he catalogued with eating, drinking, and defecating? As noted above, Luther regarded celibacy as a gift—and he warned that it was rarely given. Moreover, Luther repeatedly referred to Christ as "the inestimable gift." Christ, not sexuality, was God's unfathomable gift.

Looking through the window of history at Luther may show contemporary Christians a rather disturbing image of themselves. We rush to idealize sexuality; he did not. We learn something about Luther, but we also learn something about ourselves. Does gift-language allow Christians access to a first language of faith and its wisdom about the human person?

A Critical Appropriation of Culture

As Richard Perry and José David Rodríguez document in their chapter for this volume, culture also shapes experience. Christians should be alert to its formative power; they should be able to assess it critically. On one hand, Christians believe that the Spirit is alive, well, and working in the world. We know it is false to think that the churches contain the full range of the Spirit's movements. The Spirit works because of—and often in spite of—the churches' activities. For this reason Christians probe culture for traces of grace. They listen to stories of homosexual and heterosexual Christian couples who have struggled to be faithful to one another in a culture of self-gratification. They listen to stories of single people who want to see their sexuality as a gift to the community. They listen to the joys and struggles of people long married. We listen to these stories, sifting them for signs of the Spirit's working.

On the other hand, Christians wisely maintain a critical distance from culture. At this dawning of the new millennium, American popular culture worships sexuality. Idolatry may be difficult to distinguish from the healthy appreciation our tradition advises. When sexual practice becomes a personal entitlement or an individual right, we have crossed that line. When sexual lifestyles refuse to conform to that "most perfect marriage" between Christ and the believer, Christians need to be critical. As divorce, domestic violence, and clergy sexual misconduct plague our own churches, we need to rethink our practice of marriage. A Roman Catholic moral theologian received a barrage of critical feedback when she tried to talk normatively about sexual relations. "You can't say anything without offending someone," she sighed—and resolved to keep silent about all such matters in the future. But if all this talk about sex silences normative discussion, we are in trouble.

Christians are called to difficult and nuanced conversation about what enhances life. Jesus' final words to the lawyer at the end of the parable of the good Samaritan were after all: "Go and do likewise." Jesus' counsel allows for the lawyer to make adjustments for his own circumstances, context, and abilities. What is the way of life that conforms to this parable? Responding to that question calls for conversation with others who have accepted the challenge.

Significantly, Jesus did not invite the lawyer to "Go and do exactly what the Samaritan did." Neither did Jesus say: "Go and do whatever you want, as long as you don't hurt anyone." Particularly in matters of sexuality, it is not the case that anything goes as long as two adults give their mutual consent and no one gets hurt. These may be a standard in popular morality, but for Christians standards are more stringent. The apostle Paul struggled to break the Corinthian Christians' accommodations to their culture. "What you do with your bodies affects the body of Christ! Conform them to Christ's body." For the Corinthians, as for twenty-first century American Christians, culture retained a powerful grip on their imaginations.

Because Christians believe in a God who became flesh, a God who took on a human body, experience remains an important source of moral deliberation. Yet experience is never as innocent as it seems. Experience has always been edited, and those who would be faithful in the task of moral deliberation would be wise to inquire who the editors are.

A Sexual Ethic Shaped by Baptism: Moving from a Theological Center

In the process of moral deliberation, Scripture, tradition, reason, and experience are four sources that bear careful and critical examination. Lutherans have always accorded priority to Scripture and tradition, but they have also been unwilling to rule out the testimony of reason and experience. Rather, Lutherans have tended to use the biblical witness as a lens through which to scrutinize reason and experience for ongoing signs of the Spirit's work.

In past discussions of homosexuality, positions hardened because people were attending to one or two of the four sources to the exclusion of the others. Many cited biblical condemnations of homosexuality and the Christian tradition's refusal to recognize same-sex relations as proof positive that homosexuality should be condemned. When pressed to account for experience, they cited evidence of promiscuity and sexual instability in the gay community—a reality that needs to be addressed. But promiscuity and sexual instability are not strangers to the heterosexual community. Indeed, while the church was fiercely debating homosexuality, divorce rates spiked and sexual misconduct among heterosexual clergy and their parishioners surfaced. The question to be put to this position is whether or not the witness and churchmanship of committed and faithful couples within the gay and lesbian community might be one more sign of the Spirit's ongoing work within the world.

Others pointed to the faithful and committed relationships among gay and lesbian Christians as evidence enough that homosexuality should be supported. In referencing Scripture this group tended to overlook specific prohibitions in favor of a general appeal to neighbor-love or justice. But this group failed to be specific about a biblically based Christian sexual ethic for gays and lesbians, one that would regulate sexual behavior in the name of Christian discipleship. In absence of such a normative sexual ethic, this position looked like it was lobbying the church to give blanket affirmation to an unregulated lifestyle. This effort met with opposition, because the church does not affirm a heterosexual lifestyle. Rather, the church blesses in holy matrimony unions between men and women that conform to certain values: love of God and service to the neighbor.

One side accused the other of bending over backwards to accommodate a culture obsessed with sexuality and individualism; the other side threw back accusations of unloving, unjust, and rigid approaches to Scripture and tradition. The sexuality wars left the two sides even more entrenched than before and unable to carry on civil conversation. In his article for this volume, Daniel Olson astutely observes that various parties will not achieve a reasoned discussion of sexuality until they deal with the anger and fear generated by the conflict.

The proposal I am offering tries to find a common ground in baptism. Beginning with baptism will not calm all fronts in the sexuality wars, but it may open a safe zone for conversation. If Christians begin their discussions of sexuality with baptism, they may come up with some surprising insights. Baptism gives Christians identity, orientation, practice, and behavior unique definition. In specific, a sexual ethics informed by baptism offers some surprising insights into Christian sexual behavior. Beginning with baptism makes clear several points at the outset.

Baptism defines the Christian's "identity of primary emergency." Accordingly, a Christian's primary orientation is toward Christ. In all that he or she does, a Christian should act out of that orientation. Behavior that has as its primary objective pleasure, power, or self-discovery should be considered seriously disoriented. What a baptismal sexual ethic demands is behavior that befits members of the body of Christ.

Beginning with baptism does not endorse either homosexual or heterosexual "lifestyles." The only lifestyle a Christian should be concerned with is the lifestyle of discipleship, which is shaped by the "one flesh" union Christians have with Christ. Baptism seals that union, and the primary membership in the body of Christ informs all others. Christians who have been given that rare gift of celibacy exercise their discipleship in ways that make their union with Christ a sole and exclusive option. Others will exercise their discipleship in relationships that conform to that "most perfect marriage" they enjoy through baptism in the body of Christ.

What does making baptism a primary identity and orientation mean? Concretely, putting baptism first reminds Christians of the danger of idolatry in any sexual union. Idolatry is a danger when one partner subordinates his or her needs and desires to the other, willingly or by force, and the relationship degenerates into a kind of domestic idolatry. At times, pleasure tempts one to place one's own pleasure and self-interest above all else; at other times, it tempts one to place the pleasure and interests of the other above all else. These idolatries not only erase self and other as bounded and distinct subjects; they obscure the spiritual dimension of the relationship. A daily return to baptism keeps the believer faithful to his or her "true marriage," the union with Christ.

Making baptism an identity of primary reference raises the importance of a common spirituality in a marriage or union. Many Christians have mixed marriages: between Norwegian and Swede, between German and Irish, between Christian and Muslim, between Christian and Jew. Christian baptism may not be something the two partners share. A pastor talked about her ministry of premarital counseling: "I ask whether the two people are already living together, because the commitments involved in marriage are so different from the commitments involved in cohabitation," she remarked. "But I also ask whether the two people can pray together. Do they have some common spiritual grounding." Attending church every Sunday, even praying to the Christian God, may not be possible, but finding a common spiritual compass will be. Over time every couple needs some sort of polestar to navigate the joys and disappointments of their common life.

Finally, having baptism as a primary identity helps people find a path through the anguish of divorce, separation, or the death of a spouse or partner. Grief leaves one feeling diminished and torn from familiar moorings. Having a primary identity in baptism helps a person find a compass, as well as affording the comfort of a community of other believers.

Baptism makes sexuality a public matter. Baptism initiates Christians into a family of "the children of God." It incorporates Christians into a new community, the body of Christ. Sexuality becomes a matter of ecclesial concern: it is no longer a private matter, something that happens between two consenting adults. Sexuality has communal dimensions.

Putting baptism first reminds Christians that sex is a crowded undertaking. Actions that seem private have ripple effects in a wider world. Garrison Keillor puts this powerfully in a radio monologue about Jim, a man from the fictional town of Lake Wobegon contemplating adultery on a business trip with an attractive female colleague. Jim thinks, "although I thought my sins would be secret, they would be no more secret than an earthquake." Jim imagines a string of civic catastrophies that would occur—everything from inattentive crossing guards to unscrupulous butchers—and concludes "we all depend on each other more than we know." Even if no one ever finds out about his indiscretion, the deception required to keep it secret frays the fragile bonds of trust that make civic life possible.

Keillor's comic example imparts some serious truths. Not only are human creatures a complex integrity of body, mind, soul, and spirit, but so are human communities. What happens to one member affects the whole. In addition, Keillor's illustration underscores that people need one another to be the kind of people they have pledged to be.

Concretely, making sexuality a matter of ecclesial concern means that it is a gift and responsibility of the community. It is no longer an individual entitlement or a privacy issue. Child-rearing becomes a matter of communal concern. How do we teach our children a first language of faith? How do we instill in them respect for their bodies? How do we support and hold accountable the couples in our midst? How do we prepare people for marriage? For example, there may be irreconcilable differences between two people in relationship. Often, a community of friends, family, and fellow Christians holds them together and calls to their best selves. These jobs are too big for the pastoral team; indeed, baptism makes them the responsibility of the community.

Baptism reveals the appropriate exercise of sexuality to be within the context of a relationship shaped by promises. As creatures we flourish in relative stability. Circumstances may be beyond our control, but we do have some control over who we are in the midst of them. Promises made and kept ensure that we will be the same people tomorrow that we pledged to be today.

Because humans display a complex integrity of body, mind, soul, and spirit, what we do with our bodies sends shock waves throughout the human person. Sexual practices that neglect this—promiscuity, infidelity, narcissism, casual sex—involve more facets of the human person than the body. They kill the spirit and wound the heart. A teenager feels "dirtied" by a chance sexual encounter. What she cannot know at the time is how lasting that stain will be. Nor does she suspect that too many chance encounters will make her feel damaged for the rest of her life, not only in the eyes of others but in her own. Intimacy, an elusive but essential good, flourishes in an arena of trust and fidelity. Promise-making and promise-keeping cultivate the soil for true intimacy.

Two people cannot make enough promises to support the intimacy they crave. They depend on a community that surrounds them, making promises of its own to the couple, but also holding them in loving accountability to the pledges they have made. As Garrison Keillor put it, "We all depend on each other more than we know."

Concretely, the importance of promise-making means that Christians should pay more attention to the vows made in a ceremony. Two people promise before a community and before God. Their promises create a community of accountability. The couple publicly declares its support to a community; the community declares its support to the couple. Every marriage ceremony makes these promises implicitly, even if not every marriage lives them out. The promises of mutual accountability need to be explicit, and they need to be lived out.

The issue of whether this church will bless gay and lesbian unions raises questions for all parties. For churches and congregations, it asks whether they are willing to be communities of support for these unions in their midst. For the couples, it asks whether they are willing to support the community. A blessing from God is unconditional; a blessing from the community comes with strings.

As churches and congregations examine the issue of blessing unions, they have the opportunity to review their practice of marriage in view of the promises that surround it. Escalating rates of divorce have not left Christian communities untouched. In addition, Protestants have faced their own version of sex scandals in the church, largely between married pastors and their female parishioners. The institution of marriage needs help. Indeed, as Christians have debated homosexuality with such passion and acrimony, they may have failed to celebrate, support, and admonish the unions they had already blessed. This latest round of conversations on sexuality affords a chance to remedy that.

Values of fidelity, service, and generativity ought to direct relationships this church is prepared to support. If relationships meet these criteria, they should be supported by the church. Not all gay and lesbian unions reflect these values, nor do all heterosexual unions that the church has already blessed. Lifting up fidelity, service, and generativity raises the bar for all couples.

Sexual ethics has traditionally been quite good at telling Christians what *not* to do and less clear about what *to* do. Accordingly, teaching on sexuality has been a list of "thou shalt nots." The lifestyle of discipleship initiated in baptism offers sexual ethics a list of positive goods that direct all Christians but particularly those who have pledged to be a couple. As an ingredient in true intimacy, fidelity demands two qualities of relationships: sexual exclusivity and long-term commitment. Fidelity provides the stability humans crave in order to flourish. For Christians fidelity reflects the faithfulness shown by God in the body of Christ. As the relationship that sets the pattern for all others, membership in this body shapes our sexual relationships.

Service reflects the interdependence of Christian community. Christians are trained to notice the neighbor in need, whether that neighbor be spouse or partner, a newly widowed member struggling with solitude, or the two-thirds of the world's population living below the poverty line. Perhaps one of the concrete questions pastors should pose to engaged couples is the question of how they see their union as a form of service to near and distant neighbors.

Connected to service is the value of generativity. Most couples think of generativity in terms of procreation; they consider they have done their part by creating the next generation. Seen through the lens of baptism, however, the call to generativity claims all Christians, whether they have children or not. After all, baptism takes the issue of a sexual union and places it in the community of the children of God. In baptism the community promises to uphold, support, and nurture this new member in the faith. Generativity signals a willingness to deliver on that promise.

Many Christians, married, partnered, or single, respond by teaching Sunday school, working with youth, tutoring children. In so doing they invest in the next generation and they testify to their hope in the future. "The church has done so much for me, I wanted to give something back," a long-time Sunday school teacher remarked. Generativity is a way of "giving something back" by giving something forward. The gifts passed on are a form of service to the future.

Finally, as it has done for centuries, the church should challenge its members to restrict sexual activity to relationships that are committed and faithful. This means relationships that are sexually exclusive and long-term. These relationships build up the integrity of both the individual believer and the community. If the church decides that homosexual orientation does not disqualify one from a life of discipleship, the church should seriously consider supporting and celebrating committed and faithful unions between gay and lesbian Christians.

Both homosexual and heterosexual lifestyles should be subordinated to the lifestyle of discipleship. Membership in the body of Christ informs what Christians do with their bodies, and sexual unions should be contoured along lines suggested by the "most perfect marriage" in the body of Christ. That means restricting sexual unions to sexually exclusive, long-term relationships that pledge to embody the values of fidelity, service, and generativity.

Some will object that this conclusion opens the door to "gay marriage." Let me repeat: If this church decides that homosexual orientation does not disqualify one from a life of discipleship, the church should consider supporting committed and faithful unions in its midst. Whether the church wishes to provide liturgies solemnizing those unions is a further issue. Resolving this issue depends on the willingness of homosexual couples to be held accountable to a community of faith, as well as the community's ability to stand as a group of support, counsel, and admonition for a gay or lesbian couple. The church would be unwise to act until it has a sense of where the Spirit is leading the people of God on these two matters.

Others will object that the argument blesses gay and lesbian unions only if they conform to the model of "heterosexual marriage." Let me be very clear: The model of marriage presented does not draw on "straight" culture but rather on the culture of baptism. Christians should eschew choosing sides in this debate but find common ground in their shared calling as disciples.

In terms of sexual ethics, I think it is dangerous to create separate "homosexual" or "heterosexual" models for sexual relationships. If baptism functions as the central orientation of a Christian, a Christian sexual ethic should be equally binding on all Christians, both homosexuals and heterosexuals. The task then is to ask what kind of relationship reflects the fidelity shown us in Christ Jesus and allows us to live out our baptism in that fidelity. If we could explore baptism and its promises more deeply, we would help all people who struggle to live faithfully in a troubled world.

Discussion Questions

1. Do you find it helpful to speak of one's primary identity in baptism as the starting point for Christian sexual ethics?
2. Is promise-making important for sexual behavior? What happens when promises are broken? What does it take to sustain promises?
3. How do you as an individual and as a congregation support the marriages in your midst? If the church were to accept blessed same-sex unions, what kind of support do you think those couples would need?
4. Whether or not you have children, how do you "pay it forward"? How do you contribute to the faith formation of the next generation of Christians?
5. What conditions would have to be met theologically and ethically before the church considers blessing same-sex unions?

For Further Reading

Balch, David, ed. *Homosexuality, Science, and the "Plain Sense" of Scripture.* Grand Rapids: Eerdmans, 2000.

Cahill, Lisa. *Sex, Gender, and Christian Ethics.* Cambridge, England: Cambridge University Press, 1996.

Everett, William Johnson. *Blessed Be the Bond: Christian Perspectives on Marriage and Family.* Philadelphia: Fortress Press, 1985.

Lebacqz, Karen, and Ronald G. Barton. *Sex in the Parish.* Louisville: Westminster John Knox, 1991.

Siker, Jeffrey S., ed. *Homosexuality in the Church: Both Sides of the Debate.* Louisville: Westminster John Knox, 1994.

Wallace, Catherine M. *For Fidelity: How Intimacy and Commitment Enrich Our Lives.* New York: Alfred A. Knopf, 1998.

Notes

1. Quoted in Beverly Harrison, *Making the Connections: Essays in Feminist Social Ethics* (Boston: Beacon Press, 1985), 89. The original reference is

from Andrea Dworkin, *Woman Hating* (New York: Dutton, 1974), 22–24.

2. I thank Mark Allan Powell for this exegetical insight.

3. Martin Luther, "To the Christian Nobility of the German Nation Concerning the Reform of the Christian Estate (1520)," trans. Charles M. Jacobs, in *Luther's Works, vol. 44,* ed. James Atkinson (Philadelphia: Fortress Press, 1966), p. 177.

4. Martin Luther, "The Freedom of a Christian," in *Martin Luther's Basic Theological Writings,* ed. Timothy F. Lull (Minneapolis: Fortress Press, 1989), 603.

5. Hannah Arendt, *The Human Condition* (Chicago: University of Chicago Press, 1958), esp. 243–47.

6. Garrison Keillor, "Jim," in "News from Lake Wobegon: Spring" (Minneapolis: Minnesota Public Radio, 1983), cassette tape.

4.

We Hear in Our Own Language: Culture, Theology, and Ethics

*Richard J. Perry Jr.
and José David Rodríguez*

Now there were devout Jews from every nation under heaven living in Jerusalem. And at this sound the crowd gathered and was bewildered, because each one heard them speaking in the native language of each.

—Acts 2:5-6

Every group of people, every race, thinks about God out of its state of being, its own understanding of itself, out of its own condition of life.

—Gayraud Wilmore, *Best Black Sermons*

The influence of culture on what Christians think about God and moral behavior is hardly new to the Christian community. The mission of the church has had to interact with its cultural context since its beginning. The Pentecost story, for example, is about the beginning of the Christian church. Whenever we read that story, we are amazed at the diversity of people gathered together. As the writer tells us, the disciples, filled with the Holy Spirit, began preaching the word of God. Because of God's action through the Holy Spirit, "each one heard them speaking in the native language of each," as the New Revised Standard Version has it. We know the story and message of Jesus Christ has been shared in many ways so God's people could appropriate it through their own languages.

Throughout the history of the Christian community, many groups have sought to speak about God, Jesus Christ, the Holy Spirit, the church, ethics, and appropriate moral behavior in terms of their own experience and culture. Understanding and appreciating each group's expression of its culture is critical for the whole Christian community. Why? The depth of God's self-revelation in and through Jesus Christ shows how much God wants to draw all people to God. Certainly Paul's speech on the Areopagus (Acts 17:22-31) testifies to an attempt to relate the gospel to culture.

Our reason for beginning with the quotations above is to bring into the public arena what we may have thought privately. First, each group has a culture(s) reflecting their condition in life. And those cultures have particular worldviews.

81

We learn through our encounters with each other that our culture and worldview is limited and contains partial truth. For some groups in society, that may be a startling discovery.

Second, we realize that we are struggling with the issue of authority. How much influence should the Christian community give culture versus God's Holy Word? What, if anything, does culture contribute toward making ethical decisions and developing guidelines for appropriate moral behavior? We wonder, in the struggle, what it is that binds us together as Christians.

Third, we are standing on the shoulders of faithful people in our quest to understand the role culture plays in shaping our thoughts about God, our principles for making ethical decisions, and our standards for moral behavior. What our ancestors in the faith did, especially at the Council in Jerusalem (Acts 15), may be a model for what we may be called to do as we engage in conversation about the issue of homosexuality. So let the conversation begin.

The Enduring Problem

To further the conversation, we pose this question: In what ways does culture shape what we think about God, our principles for making ethical decisions, and our standards for moral behavior? We believe that culture, in its religious and social construction, shapes what we think, believe, and do. Culture and theology are not the same. Each culture has its own internal logic and each makes a significant contribution that enhances human knowledge and ethical wisdom. However, culture and theology are and can be related in ways that allow the Christian community to make responsible ethical decisions.

Our strategy for this conversation begins with a definition of culture. Culture is complex; yet what is attempted here is a wrestling with a universal and particular understanding of culture. We follow that discussion with a brief description of how the Christian community formulated the enduring problem between Christ and culture. This discovery is offered as a guide for framing the church's debate on homosexuality.

History is important. But we also want to discern the times in which we live. What does the church's cultural report card look like? There may be numerous ways to approach an analysis of what's going on in culture (e.g., focusing on a theme or a particular problem), and those are valid approaches. We will focus on the problem and practice of ethnocentrism. We believe ethnocentrism, the assumption of superiority of one culture over all cultures, influences both the church and broader society in their attempts at moral deliberation on homosexuality.

Next, we explore a proposal some other authors have suggested, namely, thinking of cultures as moral and behavioral laboratories. This implies a challenge to imagine and enact new moral and behavioral possibilities in our response to the opportunities and challenges presented by homosexuality. We suggest that the church's conversation on homosexuality may be better served by moving from a monocultural focus on sexual activity to a multicultural focus on gender. We will draw from the experiences of the African American and Hispanic/Latino/Latina communities to sharpen our point. Finally, we want to identify constructive contributions that make for a more just and participatory community in the debate about controversial issues, especially homosexuality.

Toward an Understanding of Culture

What is culture? Culture can be a slippery word because its definition is conditioned by a variety of social and religious experiences and social locations. The history of the word itself is varied. It could be defined as a force of power, have nationalistic overtones, or be a form of criticism.[1] The bottom line is that society and the church are full of cultures.

Some readers may ask, How can there be many cultures? We live in the United States of America and the Caribbean! There is only one culture and it is American! Those who hold this view are partially correct. There is a universal nature to culture. All cultures have, as one prominent ethicist said, "language, habits, ideas, beliefs, customs, social organization, inherited artifacts, technical processes, and values."[2] Culture serves as a way of organizing the world and socializing the human being. We are all born into a culture that existed long before our birth. Culture is a human endeavor that is continually enhanced by each generation of God's people. In the final analysis, one cannot be human without culture because culture helps us to interpret the world in which "we live and move and have our being" (Acts 17:27).

Another dimension, the religious or God-centered dimension, enhances our understanding of culture. Culture is religious or God-centered insofar as the totality of life created and lived by human beings is connected to the Triune God. The foundation of culture is its religious nature expressed in various forms. Accordingly, "religion is the substance of culture, culture is the form of religion."[3] Culture, we suggest, is *a meaning-giving system created by a particular group of people that expresses, forms, and transmits, in culturally specific forms, how the people and all things are connected to God.* Art, language, literature, songs, folk stories, and proverbs provide concrete forms for religious, theological, ethical, and moral wisdom. As cultures encounter each other—a dynamic process in itself—the forms change and new forms are adopted. The continuous task facing the Christian community is how to answer the enduring problem of the relationship between Christ and culture.

Answering the Enduring Problem

Scholars have given a number of different accounts of how the Christian community has struggled with the tension between Christ and culture. Some have focused on a sociological analysis of how the forms the church has taken express a reaction to the culture as demonstrated, for example, in the contrast between a mainline church and a sect. Others have identified certain theological motifs that appear in some era of history.

Among the many voices is that of prominent German-American ethicist H. Richard Neibuhr. In *Christ and Culture* he outlines five responses by the Christian community. The "Christ against Culture" approach seeks a withdrawal from society and the influence of culture. By contrast, the "Christ of Culture" position seeks an accomodation between Christian faith and the best of human culture. "Christ above Culture" wants to be involved in the cultural life of society but place it under the direction of the church's teaching and influence. "Christ and Culture in Paradox" seeks to recognize the relationship as one of tension. The final response, "Christ Transforming Culture," typically seeks to convert culture to the will of God. While sometimes blurred, these distinctions are useful in gathering the history of the Christian community's engagement of culture into some type of order.

Where are Lutherans in this schema? We have traditionally understood that Christ and culture are paradoxically related. The tension is framed as a choice between God and human beings. Grace comes from God, and sin is in humans. The paradoxical Christian contends that all Christians are redeemed sinners. Christ and culture are authorities the Christian is called to obey, with the knowledge that God saves them through Christ in the midst of a sinful culture. These overlapping spheres of influence exist under God's rule. And as such each is relatively autonomous, with its own values and beliefs. Christians exist in culture and cannot be extricated from it. Culture cannot save us because salvation is received through God's grace incarnated in Jesus Christ. Culture is filled with sin and thus ruled by God's law.

The Lutheran tradition interacts with culture especially in its descriptive and interpretative task. When Lutheran theology and ethics engage with culture, our understandings of all three are changed. Lutherans would normally understand that theology, ethics, and culture are dynamic human processes. Because these are human endeavors, they are filled with sin, yet they offer the possibility of growing through our encounter with the Word of God and with culture. Individuals, shaped by a living and dynamic understanding of God and Jesus Christ, influence culture through their vocation or calling as believers. Professor James Nestingen's essay in this volume summarizes a Lutheran understanding of the law, the gospel, and the life of the believer and its goal, namely, service to the neighbor.

We suggest that the Lutheran tradition has understood and managed this enduring problem in only a partial and limited way. Until recently, it has reflected one culture's understanding of God, Jesus Christ, the Holy Spirit, and the church. For example, the "orders of creation" doctrine, which holds that God created the family, government, church, and economics, is a key theological insight for Lutherans. However, from a monocultural perspective we are left with a static understanding of those "orders." These forms are universal, they are biblically based, God ordained them, and, consequently, they are unchangeable. Again, James Nestingen nicely describes how these "orders" work in Lutheran thinking, using the key word *relationships*. And these relationships are carried out in service to the neighbor. But the question emerges: What other types of relationships can be, and in fact are, established within those orders?

A Critique of Culture

Here, though, we take a slightly different direction. Since the mid-1960s a universal or monocultural understanding of culture, theology, and ethics has come under critique. This critique, offered in most cases by new voices—those of African Americans, Asians/Pacific Islanders, Latinas/Latinos, Native Americans, and women—has enlarged the conversation. The central critique is the lack of particularity. While all cultures contain what we identified earlier as culture, one cannot speak of culture generally. One always has to speak of a multitude of cultures in their particularity.

This interplay between the universal and the particular is evident in the many forms an ethical principle is shared. We can all agree, as Christians, that universal ethical wisdom is shared through the Ten Commandments, biblical proverbs, the person and work of Jesus Christ, the Sermon on the Mount, and stories about biblical heroes and heroines. However, the interpretation and application of this ethical wisdom is shaped by a group's experience in the world.

In her chapter in this volume, Professor Martha Stortz provides a helpful view of human experience as a source for theology and ethics. The components of experience (i.e., language and culture critically appropriated) shape us; yet we still look for God's saving word of grace in language and culture. We agree that one should listen to the stories of homosexual and heterosexual Christian people as well as the stories of the multitude of cultures. In other words, Lutherans want to embrace the stories because the Holy Spirit may be leading us into a newer and deeper understanding of God's grace.

Our listening and gathering of various stories opens us to a multitude of ways in which racial/ethnic communities share ethical wisdom. Those stories provide a vehicle through which moral behavior was, and is, taught and transmitted to young people. It is commonly understood that the great majority of African Americans experience racism and racial discrimination. In order to combat these experiences, ethical wisdom is shared through stories and proverbs. For example, in recent decades a common ethical saying in African American culture was "God don't like ugly." This theological and ethical saying, articulated in vernacular, combines the apostle Paul's words about reaping what you sow and the African American community's perception of their condition in society. As a child of the living God, you were expected always to act in a Christlike manner. There was no greater scolding than being reminded that "God don't like ugly" when you began to act contrary to how you were trained or how the community expected you to act. Acting contrary to one's "home training" and/or religious upbringing risks bringing dishonor and shame on the family and community. Such behavior made the family and community vulnerable to the evils of society. Consequently, one has a dual accountability to God and the community. As noted at the beginning of this chapter, what one says about God, Jesus Christ, the Holy Spirit, and standards for governing moral behavior emerges from the concrete experience of a group over space and time.

The diversity of cultures in American society has, for example, broadened our understanding of who and what constitutes a family. Once upon a time, a family consisted of a mother, father, and children. Yet over time, our understanding of family has changed. Childless couples, divorcees, foster parents, single parents, and single people also can constitute a "family." And in some cultures, the family includes more than parents and children; it includes extended family members. Thus, the family as one of the "orders of creation" is a dynamic doctrine, open to how God through the Holy Spirit might be doing something new in and through the diversity of cultures in society. Similarly, an alternate view of culture is necessary for the church's conversation on the issue of homosexuality to move beyond a monocultural focus to a multicultural focus. What is going on in society that contributes to such high emotion regarding the issue of homosexuality?

Discerning the Signs of the Times

What does our church's report card look like? A careful analysis of our contemporary era tells us several things. First, some would say we are living on moral fragments. What formerly was perceived as the center of our faith, namely, the crucified and risen Jesus Christ, has lost its hold on believing Christians. Some people no longer remember the central story of the Bible. And those institutions normally responsible for forming individuals and communities—the family and the church—have failed in their primary responsibilities. This may be attributed to the rise of self-serving individualism as the only moral compass.

Second, some people believe that because various cultures in our society have found their voices, what was once considered uniform about what constitutes being a American and a Christian has been reduced to a form of "tribalism." The emergence of a diversity of cultures, and the mores they contribute to society and the church, leads some people to believe that we have a new form of relativism. Consequently, there are no principles for judging behavior. Society has lost its religious, theological, and ethical norms. It's difficult, they say, to make any judgments without a common center.

Third, our society has at least two attitudes about the issue of sex and sexuality, one private and the other public. On the one hand, sex and sexuality is considered a private matter. It is better left in the domain of the home. One implication of this is a repressed expression of sexuality. Sex, sexuality, and the body are viewed negatively. On the other hand, our society glorifies sexuality, notably through the advertising, movie, and music industries. Some scholars argue that this glorification of sexuality is driven by our market economy.

A fourth factor we still face in society and church is the matter of race. For many people this is a difficult subject to talk about because so many groups see, understand, and experience the reality of life differently. This difficulty is riddled with painful histories. Accordingly, it is difficult for groups to trust each other when they have been subjected to racially charged experiences and treatment by the dominant society.

These four symptoms may reveal that one of the marks of the contemporary era is its lack of memory. What guides a monocultural view of society and its ethical principles is the normative character of the dominant culture. The leading ideology since the founding of the United States has been the idea of the "melting pot." It has been assumed that all groups who live in America would lose their cultural distinctiveness and embrace a new culture, identity, and set of values called "American."

This ideology, we believe, is sustained by a more fundamental spiritual and cultural crisis, a form of sin grounded in a tragic form of ethnocentrism. The rise of ethnocentrism speaks to our society and church's inability to engage difference.

We in America have learned a lesson well. We are great mask-wearers. We smile yet our hearts race when we encounter the "other." Our blood pressure rises because the poor and marginalized in society challenge what the dominant culture assumes are universal principles and values. But mask-wearing is as complex as culture and is practiced for multiple reasons. For some in the dominant culture, masks cover up contempt for those who are different. This type of mask-wearing is anchored in hierarchical power that enforces its own view.

To be sure, there is a positive dimension to ethnocentrism. All cultures must celebrate their own accomplishments. And all cultures must develop, critique, refine, and transmit what it considers appropriate moral behavior to its members. The form of ethnocentrism we want to challenge is the assumption that the dominant culture is the standard for judging the morality of all others. The dominant culture has become so impressed with its own religious, theological, cultural, and ethical heritage, its own freedom and power, that it forgets that it is stifling other cultures. Thus, its homogenizing practices emphasize subordination of other people based on their difference. If there is one thing the aftermath of September 11 clearly testifies to, it is the rise of this sensibility that "our" American culture is superior! Racial profiling—perceiving a person or group as threatening based on their appearance, religious practices, or mode of dress—is a tragic expression of ethnocentrism.

On the other hand, people of color wear masks for other reasons—sometimes simply to survive with a dominant culture that rejects them and renders them invisible. Accordingly, as the prominent African American cultural critic and philosopher W. E. B. Du Bois describes so aptly, one develops a sense of "twoness." That is, one always views and measures oneself through the eyes of the dominant culture and through one's own eyes. The "other" (whether categorized by race, sexual orientation, class, or ethnic background) is under the constant stress of seeking approval from the dominant culture.

The import of this moral paradox has led to numerous responses by people of color. One response is assimilation. The assimilationist assumes that whatever may be the difference between people and cultures (i.e., race, sexual orientation, class, and ethnicity) can be overcome by conformity to the dominant culture. Assimiliationists have been made to feel and think their culture is inferior and fails to contribute to what the Christian community thinks about God, ethics, and appropriate moral behavior. Said differently, they give up the particularity of their culture for the dominant culture's worldview, values, and norms. While there is a desire to be known "by the content of their character," what the dominant culture decides constitutes character is embraced by all the cultures.

An Alternative Proposal for Understanding Culture

The critique of a monocultural view of what we think about God, ethics, and moral behavior raises the need to explore the relationship between cultural particularity and universal humanity. Many African Americans, Latinos/Latinas, Asians/Pacific Islanders, and Native Americans consider this one of the central issues today. The fundamental question raised by this perspective lies in understanding the process leading to assimilation into mainstream society. The dominant expression of assimilation presupposes a one-way process of cultural change to a white, middle-class norm.[4] Recent studies by representatives of racially and culturally diverse communities are proposing alternative modes of cultural transformation intrinsic to the processes of collective identity formation.

Rather than begin with a monocultural view of society and church, a result of the "melting pot" theory and its insistence on "color blindness" and the universality of ethical norms, scholars are suggesting that we begin with a multicultural perspective. Basic to this perspective are two points. First, cultures function as more than mere depositories of behavioral and moral knowledge. Cultures also function as laboratories in the service of creating economic, social, and political equity between different groups in society. All cultures, in their particularity, shape their members in what is considered appropriate behavior and gender roles.

Second, as African Americans, Asians/Pacific Islanders, Latinos/Latinas, and Native Americans recover their own heritages and share them with the wider society, society and the church will grow in their understanding of the complexity of the world. While this may appear to be "tribalism," in America the act of recovering one's heritage is more an act of complementing the story of all groups living in the United States and the Caribbean. As groups encounter each other, they learn new and different ways of being that may enhance their ability to flourish in society.[5]

Gaining a multicultural perspective is a complex process. This process is conditioned by the location of the individual subject and the group as well as the economic, historical, social, and cultural forces with which they interact. Therefore, it also requires a determined and intentional effort.

Yet we believe that this perspective not only contributes to the common well-being of society as a whole but also is conducive to the human's spiritual, moral, and intellectual growth. Multicultural insight is particularly important when we are confronted with perplexing challenges that need more creative and constructive responses than those traditionally offered. For us, this is precisely the case when the church explores its response to the challenge of homosexuality as a community of faith committed to the witness of the gospel in its continual task of moral discernment.

In an earlier book, *The Promise of Lutheran Ethics*, contemporary Lutheran ethicists responded to the invitation of helping members of the Evangelical Lutheran Church in America to reflect on the challenges that the church and the world face today. Their specific task was to engage in a common effort to clarify the basic dimensions of what constitutes Lutheran ethics. A reflection on the collective contribution of these various authors led the book's editors to highlight the need to resist the unbridled individualism and the exploitation of people and of creation that are characteristic of our contemporary society. To develop a common project of moral discernment in which shared theological understandings and dynamics could lead toward the common good, a multitude of viewpoints participated.[6] For example, one essay on African American Lutheran ethical agency reflected on how this group embraces and expresses what it means to be Christian and Lutheran.[7]

In reflecting on the significance of these contributions to the topic of homosexuality, we want to probe more deeply in two areas. First, the experience of diverse cultural groups in addressing the presence of homosexuals in their own communities is vital to our conversation. Second, the theological perspectives emerging from these diverse cultural communities may enrich those of the traditionally dominant white male heterosexual communities. The presence of homosexuals themselves in the debate, in our common effort to become a community of moral discernment in faithfulness to the gospel, would reveal how the multiple viewpoints are more complementary than divisive.

Preliminary Considerations of the Issue of Homosexuality from the Perspective of People of Color

The church serves as an important institution in the lives of people of color. Contrary to what many people may say or think, in various racial and ethnic communities, the church is the anchor. It has served and continues to serve as a place where leadership is developed and exercised, and where many poor people are affirmed as God's people. The church, in many of these communities, has served and continues to serve as a voice for social and moral reform. Yet when it comes to the issue of homosexuality, these communities' attitudes and beliefs appear to be the same as the dominant culture's. Some of these churches refuse to acknowledge the presence of homosexual persons and preach that it is an abomination before the Lord.

Like many of the dominant culture's own vigorous advocates and critics of homosexuality, people of color consult the Bible to support their diverse views on the subject. Some of them simply hold that the Bible says homosexuality and homosexual acts are wrong. Others read it as inconclusive about the whole matter. What is going on here? Is this simply a desire of people of color to assimilate and not appear outside the mainstream of biblical thinking?

In the African American community, these questions illustrate the complexity and plurality of thinking on what the Bible has to say about the issue of homosexuality. The Bible is authoritative in the African American community! It is authoritative insofar as the biblical stories contribute to the movement from oppression to freedom. Professor Mark Powell's chapter on the Bible is critically important because he outlines in summary fashion many of the arguments employed against homosexuality. Yet we would contend some of those arguments are culturally conditioned.

Although in the early and painful history of African American people in the Americas they were prohibited from reading the Bible, they later read it because it provided a language and worldview that could be embraced as they negotiated existence in the Americas. If God could deliver Daniel from the lion's den, surely God would deliver African American people from their oppression. Thus, the life condition of African American people provides the lens through which the Bible is interpreted.

Strong in the memory of the African American community is how the Bible was used to maintain systems of slavery and racial discrimination. While some in our contemporary era may find it hard to believe things were as bad as they were in the seventeenth, eighteenth, and nineteenth centuries, stories are emerging that tell riveting episodes of what slave owners did to slaves. Included in those stories are poignant examples of how African American people were taken advantage of sexually. In other words, their bodies were not under their control.

The church in the African American experience took on the responsibility of transmitting a biblically based understanding of God and humankind that counteracted the stereotypes and sexually negative stereotypes of African American women and men. The church in the African American community developed a canon that provided a canopy over the people. Said differently, since the African American church could not trust slave owners' interpretation of the Bible, the church appropriated those texts that enhance a community's life chances (e.g., Gal. 3:28). Thus, any interpretation of the Bible emerging from outside the African American community was, and still is today, suspect.

This is precisely the story told by homosexual persons within the many cultures of society. As Professor Daniel Olson's chapter describes eloquently, scientists have been able to identify some of the causes of anger in people. In the case of homosexuals, the church has sometimes contributed to their anger. While the African American church, for example, has embraced biblical texts that exhort the freedom of God's people, when it comes to the homosexual community, the church fails to include them in God's liberating activity.

The same dilemma that occurs within biblical interpretation—namely, failing to take into account culture or race—appears in other disciplines. While the cross-cultural anthropological and historical literature that studies the topic of homosexuality is extensive, there are comparatively few resources that explore the intersection of race with sexuality and homosexuality. Many stories are being shared of how homosexuals within the multicultural community receive support neither from their own community nor from the dominant culture. For any church denomination to get beyond the emotions of the issue of homosexuality, it must appreciate the differences between empathetic, vigilant, and critical listening, as Olson has identified them.

Ironically, most newly emerging historical and anthropological research supports the belief that homosexual conduct and identity are socially constructed. Yet there is comparatively little contemporary research on the differences between homosexuals of color and the dominant culture, especially regarding the way they integrate their sexual and ethnic identities into their daily lives. We are aware that the family network can also hinder the affirmation of homosexual identity of individuals of every cultural background. There are an increasing number of studies that show how family is important in affirming the value of individuals regardless of their gender identity.

Significantly, these studies reveal more tolerant attitudes about homosexual conduct and identity from the perspectives of these various communities. They also tell of the resources and social networks among people of color in the tolerance and support of homosexual identity; among these are the family and other communal networks. While Latino families, like most other families in the United States, presuppose a heterosexual orientation, studies comparing them with other ethnic groups on tolerance of homosexuality show that the Latino extended family system, with its broader networks of support and cooperation, allows individuals more flexibility in affirming their homosexual identity.

In his study of the social and ethical implications of the family, religion, and other communal networks for Latinos in the United States, Ismael García argues for an alternative way of moral thinking as a contribution of this community in developing a more diverse and inclusive society of moral discernment. The model proposed by García emphasizes the notions of recognition and care. This model accentuates the needs of people over principles, and prioritizes the role of ethics for enhancing the goodness of our life together. The model further establishes familial and group relationships as morally more significant than abstract principles and conceptions of justice, and places the moral systems of subcultural groups as normatively more relevant than universal standards of ethics. This emphasis on recognition and care manifests a commitment of love for the powerless and excluded within a loveless society that frustrates the aspirations of its culturally different members. The ethics of recognition and care also protects and empowers us to be the unique people that we are. It does so by promoting as a primary concern transforming the conditions of oppression, prejudice, domination, and injustice experienced by our people. Again, Olson's chapter is helpful because one cannot converse with those who are racially, ethnically, or sexually different if one is engaged in "vigilant listening," projecting negative attributes or launching personal attacks.

Gender and Sexual Orientation as Cultural Constructions

A multicultural perspective, as it relates to our conversation about homosexuality, implies a new understanding of gender and sexual orientation. Increasingly, scholars—whether we agree with them or not—are suggesting that gender, in contrast to sex, represents both a cultural category and a dynamic process of socialization. While sex is a reference to human biology, gender is defined and determined by human culture. As a process of socialization, gender follows the ongoing formation of a culture. Consequently, as cultures change, they modify their definition of gender.

In the context of the United States, the political, economic, and ideological structure that privileges the superiority of the white male creates and perpetuates negative stereotypes for the rest of the human community. For African American men, the internalization of this standard can have negative and onerous consequences in their own lives and in the lives of those around them. A resistance to this stereotype requires the willingness to embrace a new standard of what it means to be a black heterosexual male in this society.[8]

Similarly, African American women and their bodies have been denigrated by the dominant culture. Many distorted stereotypes were created in an attempt to justify the contradiction between sexual and physical mistreatment and the espoused values of being "Christian." African American women were seen as sexually aggressive, promiscuous, and lacking in the moral virtue characteristic of "normal" women. In sum, what we think about one's sexuality is a process that includes both biology and culture.

A multicultural perspective also may entail reconstructing the meaning of gender. Focusing on gender requires the retrieval of both cultural and theological legacies constitutive of the various communities. For example, within the African American community it means highlighting the communal nature of the West African legacy, which gives African American men and women a sense of respect based on how well they participate, take care of, and share in the African American family.

The theological legacy provides the spiritual foundation of God's gracious and unconditional transformative expression of love, uniquely manifested in the redemptive ministry of Jesus Christ, leading to the ongoing struggle toward inclusive and holistic liberation and the practice of freedom. This means capturing a stronger sense of what it means to be created in the image of God.

Conclusion

As we engage in this moral deliberation, helping our church respond to the topic of homosexuality as our witness of faith, we suggest the following considerations. First, voices from our nondominant ethnic communities should be incorporated. Even the present effort to address this concern limits the perspective to the authors selected for this project. Surely one of the crucial absent voices is one representing the homosexual community. We need to embrace cultural diversity as a resource that nourishes our moral and intellectual growth.

Second, as we venture to engage with new issues and circumstances, we need to develop attitudes and alternatives that recognize and care for those subject to prejudice and exclusion. Our inability to understand or support the experience of others cannot justify the denial of their human dignity, or of their legitimate claims. Our lack of knowledge betrays our own limitations, not the conditions of those whom we are unable to accept or support. This lack of understanding may be better addressed by further study and dialogue with those we disagree with, rather than excluding or expressing our prejudice against them. This is a responsibility we have, regardless of how we feel about specific questions like the blessing of same-sex unions or the ordination of persons in such committed unions.

Finally, our commitment to venture into a communal effort of moral discernment on this topic from the perspective of faith makes certain demands on us. As noted by some scholars from the multicultural community, our belief in the spiritual foundation of God's gracious and unconditional transformative expression of love, uniquely manifested in the redemptive ministry of Jesus Christ, should bestow on us a sense of freedom for dialogue, even with those who differ from our own experience and convictions. Let this freedom in the gospel of God pierce through our most extreme fears, our unreasonable doubts and our predisposed apprehensions, so that we may deliberate with one another in all our diversity as members of the same baptismal community.

Discussion Questions

1. Why is it important to consider the role of culture in theological and ethical discussions and formulations?
2. What are three important reasons emphasized in this chapter for considering the relationship between gospel and culture?
3. What are some of the important contributions of African-American, Latino,

and other ethnic cultures to our moral and theological deliberations on homosexuality?

4. When different cultures within the church have different perspectives on certain issues, is that a problem or an opportunity for greater understanding?

For Further Reading

The Greatest Taboo: Homosexuality in Black Communities. Constantine-Simms, Delroy, ed. Foreword by Henry Louis Gates Jr. Los Angeles and New York: Alyson Publications, 2001.

Douglas, Kelly Brown. *Sexuality and the Black Church: A Womanist Perspective.* Maryknoll, New York: Orbis Books, 1999.

Garcia, Ismael. *Dignidad: Ethics through Hispanic Eyes.* Nashville: Abingdon, 1997, 21–75.

Greene, Beverly. "Family, Ethnic Identity, and Sexual Orientation: African-American Lesbians and Gay Men." In *Lesbian, Gay, and Bisexual Identities in Families: Psychological Perspectives.* Edited by Charlotte J. Patterson and Anthony R. D'Augelli. New York: Oxford University Press, 1998, 40–52.

Hopkins, Dwight N. "A New Black Heterosexual Male." *Voices from the Third World,* 24, no. 1 (June 2001).

Men of Color: A Context for Service to Homosexually Active Men. New York: Harrington Park Press, 1996.

Moya, Paula M. L., "Cultural Particularity versus Universal Humanity." Jorge J. E. Gracia and Pablo De Greiff, eds., *Hispanics/Latinos in the United States: Ethnicity, Race, and Rights.* New York: Routledge, 2000.

Notes

1. Kathryn Tanner, *Theories of Culture: A New Agenda for Theology* (Minneapolis: Fortress Press, 1997), 6–16.

2. H. Richard Niebuhr, *Christ and Culture* (New York: Harper and Row, 1951), 32.

3. Paul Tillich, *Theology of Culture* (London: Oxford University Press, 1959), 42.

4. Jorge J. E. Gracia and Pablo De Greiff, *Hispanics/Latinos in the United States: Ethnicity, Race, and Rights* (New York: Routledge, 2000), 1–20.

5. Paula M. L. Moya, "Cultural Particularity versus Human Universality," in *Hispanics/Latinos in the United States,* 90.

6. Karen L. Bloomquist and John R. Stumme, eds., *The Promise of Lutheran*

Ethics (Minneapolis: Fortress Press, 1998), 1–10.

7. Richard J. Perry Jr., "African American Lutheran Ethical Action: The Will to Build," in *The Promise of Lutheran Ethics*, 75–96.

8. Dwight N. Hopkins, "A New Black Heterosexual Male," *Voices from the Third World 24, no. 1* (June 2001): 25–28.

5.

Talking about Sexual Orientation: Experience, Science, and the Mission of the Church

Daniel L. Olson

It's one of the "culture wars." You can tick them off: The death penalty, gun control, abortion, stem cell research, human cloning, *sexual orientation* . . . the list goes on and on. These are the issues that presently polarize the American public and provide an endless supply of grist for the popular media mill.

The culture wars have polarized the churches too. Sometimes it seems that many Christians today see their mission as taking a position on one of the culture wars and then bringing the authority of God to bear on the task of winning the war. Is that the mission of the church? If not, how does the mission of the church relate to our discussions in our congregations and synods of issues related to sexual orientation? How is God's mission to the world best served by the church as it faces this present crisis?

How, and to Whom, Should We Listen?

Attentive listening comes in different shapes: empathetic listening, vigilant listening, and critical listening are three very distinct activities. Each affects differently the one who listens, the one who is listened to, and the relationship between them.

Empathetic listening is required of one who would nurture friendships or care for the well-being of loved ones. A friend celebrating an achievement, a heartbroken child—both need someone with an empathetically attuned ear. Without it the friendship will wither; the developing child will fail to thrive. When one listens empathetically, one seeks to "tune in" to the inner experience of another person.

Vigilant listening is required of one who guards the perimeter of a camp in a war zone. A vigilant listener must be ready to attack, defend, freeze, or sound the alarm, all without the benefit of a moment's notice. In such a situation, if empathetic listening were possible, it would be dangerous. However, the basic design of the human mind probably makes empathetic listening impossible in such a situation.

Critical listening is most appropriate for one inquiring about scientific advances, listening to a lecture, acquiring new information, or learning a skill. Critical listening is mindful of the tentative state of all human knowledge. In a situation that calls for critical listening, empathy for the lecturer, the author, or the scientist is merely a distraction. In a situation that calls for critical listening, vigilant listening is likely to be an obstacle to learning.

I have been doing a lot of listening to listeners in the church lately, and it appears that we may have our listening styles mixed up. Much of the listening seems to be of the vigilant sort—the kind that is crucial in a war zone. When that happens, empathetic listening and critical listening become casualties. Clarity of thought and cohesiveness of community also become casualties.

Which of these forms of listening will we engage in at any given time? That will be determined by what is motivating us to listen. And what will motivate us to listen? That will depend on the context in which we believe ourselves to be. Nurturing a friendship, guarding a camp in a war zone, taking notes in a lecture—those are very different contexts. They motivate very different styles of listening. The point is critical and bears repetition: (1) *how* we listen is always affected by our *motivation* for listening, and (2) our *motivation* for listening is always determined by our understanding of the *context* in which we listen.

The Context of Our Listening: A Community Called into Mission

We all recall the old riddles of our childhood.

Q: When is a door not a door?
A: When it's ajar (a jar).

Q: When is a dog's tail not a dog's tail?
A: When it's a wagon (wagging).

Q: When is the church not the church?
A: When it has forgotten its mission.

That last one is not a joke. At the heart of the identity of the Christian church is its mission. The risen Lord entrusts his followers with stewardship of the mission that he came to accomplish. But to the commission that he gives, Jesus adds a caveat: he cautions his disciples not to undertake their mission until they have been "clothed with power from on high" (Luke 24:49). In John's Gospel, when the risen Jesus meets the apostles for the first time, he says to them, "As the Father sent me, so I send you." Immediately he breathes on them and says, "Receive the Holy Spirit" (John 20:21-22). We must note well the close connection between Jesus bestowing mission and Jesus bestowing the Holy Spirit on his followers. Whatever the mission of the church is, it is clearly not a matter of "doing what comes naturally." It isn't even a matter of doing what is extremely difficult. It seems likely that if Jesus had merely given his disciples a task that was very difficult, he would have said, "Try very hard." If he had merely given them a task that was very dangerous, he might have said, "Have courage." But Jesus said to those whom he commissioned with his mission, "Receive the Holy Spirit."

Jesus asked his disciples this question: "What more are you doing than others?" (Matthew 5:47). He didn't address that question to individual believers but to a gathered community of disciples. He wasn't asking them to describe some outstanding personal quality or heroic individual effort that made them superior to other individuals. Nor was he asking them to describe some aspect of their life together as a community of faith that let them claim superior status in relation to other religious communities. Quite the contrary: In the Gospels, Jesus reminds his followers repeatedly of the critical necessity for them to cultivate humility within themselves as individuals and among themselves as a community.

When Jesus inquired, "What more are you doing than others?" he was asking his followers to think about how their life together in community would bear witness to him as their Lord and the Lord of all creation. Jesus was talking to his disciples about the mission for which they were to be empowered: they were to live their life together as a community that was to bear his name in the world.

When Jesus asks his disciples this question, he isn't putting others down or describing bad things that others are doing: he is describing some of the very best things in life. He is talking about greeting each other with a smile. He is talking about being part of a circle of friends in which invitations to dinner are reciprocated. He is talking about empathetic attunement to family members and compassion for friends. Jesus is talking about the best parts of human nature. And he is not saying that there is anything wrong with any of these: all of these are clearly gifts from God that should be celebrated. It's just that reciprocating a dinner invitation, smiling in response to a friendly smile, and enjoying a lively conversation with someone who shares your opinions about important issues—none of these will do much to transform a human community faced with a predicament that it cannot solve, a predicament that could very well lead to the self-destruction of the entire human community. That is a possibility that we are all too frequently reminded of at the beginning of the twenty-first century.

When Jesus asks his disciples, "What more are you doing than others?" he isn't calling for greater quantity but for a different *quality*. He isn't saying, "You should be doing all of the good things that you and others ordinarily do, but you should be doing them with more frequency and with greater intensity." Jesus is saying, "I call on you to exceed the built-in limits of the wonderful things that you and all other people do naturally." In all likelihood, that would require being "clothed with power from on high."

Empathy is part of human nature; some would say it is the best part of human nature. But empathy runs flat up against limits. And when empathy reaches its limits, beyond those limits there is no limit to the human capacity for cruelty. Those who orchestrated the Holocaust were empathetic to friends and compassionate to family members, but they had defined Jews and certain others in a way that put them beyond the limits of empathy, and they felt no dissonance in orchestrating a wholesale extermination. When Jesus asked his disciples, "What more are you doing than others?" he was calling them to extend empathetic understanding and compassionate caring beyond the limits that human nature places upon it: "I say to you, Love your enemies and pray for those who persecute you" (Matt. 5:43-44). He called his followers to extend their hospitality beyond the delightful circles of reciprocal invitations: "When you give a luncheon or a dinner, do not invite your friends or your brothers or your relatives or rich neighbors, in case they may invite you in return, and you would be repaid. But when you give a banquet, invite the poor, the crippled, the lame, and the blind. And you will be blessed, because they cannot repay you, for you will be repaid at the resurrection of the righteous" (Luke 14:12-14).

In all of this, Jesus is describing the mission that he entrusts to his followers. But note well: This aspect of their mission applies to their relationships with each other within the community of faith. Jesus is not here describing things that we are to go and do elsewhere among other people in other places. He's talking about the way we relate to each other—thoughtless, ornery, abrasive, and downright obnoxious as we all sometimes are—within the local congregation. Now a mission like that just might require being "clothed with power from on high."

Since Jesus describes the mission of his followers in terms of things that human beings are not innately motivated to do, it is endlessly tempting to explain away this part of our mission. If only we can define "mission" as something that happens in other places, then we can be done with it by contributing money to send other people to other places and support them while they are there. But we could probably do that rather easily without being "clothed with power from on high." When Jesus called upon his followers to be his witnesses, it is clear that he sent them out to make authentic and persuasive verbal presentations of the gospel message to others. But it is equally clear that speaking the gospel message to others was not the only witness Jesus expected of his followers, or even the most important one. It was also through the quality of their life together that they were to witness to the transforming power of the gospel. It was through living together as a community in a way that transcended the built-in limits on empathy, compassion, and forgiveness that his followers were to witness to Jesus. Clearly, to do that requires receiving the Holy Spirit.

I believe that the mission of the church in our present discussion of sexual orientation is this: to demonstrate to the world that it is possible, through the power of the Holy Spirit, to disagree vigorously about important, emotionally charged issues without attacking one another in moral indignation and without turning away from one another in moral disgust. I believe that there are some persuasive biblical reasons for claiming that this is a significant dimension of our mission as Christ's church at this time, in this place.

The seventeenth chapter of John's Gospel has come to be known as Jesus' "High Priestly Prayer." As Jesus prepares to go out from the place where he has eaten the Passover with his disciples (he is about to go to Gethsemane—and from there to Calvary), he prays for his followers in their life together. Now when people start repeating themselves, we get a sense of what is really important to them. Jesus repeats himself no fewer than *four times* in this prayer! (Remember, according to Matthew 6:7, Jesus warned his disciples not to engage in endless repetition in their prayers). But this is what the Fourth Gospel reports Jesus to have prayed for as he prepared to go to his death:

"that they may be one, as we are one" (John 17:11)
"that they may all be one" (John 17:21)
"that they may be one, as we are one" (John 17:22)
"that they may become completely one" (John 17:23)

And why was Jesus so concerned about the unity of his followers?

Was it because Jesus knew that our deepest human needs can be met only if we live together in community? Or maybe it was because he believed that his disciples would be happier and more fulfilled if they got along with each other. Perhaps Jesus just wanted his individual followers to strengthen and support one another in their individual faith journeys. Well, we don't have to guess about this one—the correct answer is "None of the above."

Jesus states clearly the reason for his oft-voiced concern for the unity of his followers. It was through their unity that they would fulfill their mission to the world: "I pray that they may all be one, in order that the world might know that you have sent me" (John 17:21); "I pray that they may become completely one, in order that the world might believe that you have sent me" (John 17:23). In what does that unity consist? Is it merely an organizational thing? Is it the unity of a community of like-minded people? Are we called to be a community of shared experience? The answer to all of these options must be an emphatic "No!"

The church is not a community of like-minded people. Communities of the like-minded are a dime a dozen. I belong to a number of communities of like-minded people, and they enhance my experience of life. But communities of the like-minded are at best innocuous and merely ignore the otherwise-minded. Sometimes they become arrogant and look down on the otherwise-minded. At their worst, communities of the like-minded become demonic and condemn the otherwise-minded. There are plenty of communities of like-minded people to fulfill anybody's need for spending time with people who share their interests.

And there are far too many communities of like-minded people who despise those who are otherwise-minded. Communities of like-minded people are not identified anywhere in the Bible as playing a significant role in furthering God's intentions for the world that God loves. It in no way requires being "clothed with power from on high" to form and maintain a community of the like-minded, and communities of the like-minded in no way serve as transforming agents in God's world. What the world needs to see is a community that can sustain its unity in the midst of disagreement over emotionally charged issues, without demonizing or disregarding, excluding or humiliating each other. The present situation provides the church with a magnificent opportunity to really be the church: to genuinely disagree and differ about really important things while steadfastly refusing to turn away from one another in disgust or attack one another in righteous indignation.

Of course, we may decide that the best thing to do is to divide ourselves into two separate communities of like-minded people. We may decide to turn away from one another in disgust or attack one another in moral indignation. We may simply abandon the effort to talk to each other or listen to each other. We may decide to go our separate ways over this issue. If history repeats itself, that is the most likely outcome of our present discussion about homosexuality. And, while it may be important to try to keep the Evangelical Lutheran Church in America together, the survival of the ELCA is not a matter of *ultimate* importance. The *mission* that our Lord has entrusted to us *is*, however, a matter of *ultimate importance*. And if we simply decide to form two separate communities of like-minded people, what will be our answer to the question that Jesus put to his disciples: "What more are you doing than others?"

A "Hot-Button Issue": Is Listening Possible?

Sexual orientation is a "hot-button issue" in the church today. It evokes in many people the sudden surge of anger that has come to be called "flash-anger." I have interviewed many people in the process of gathering information for this chapter, and I have experienced flash-anger coming at me from both directions. Flash-anger is the kind of anger that surges suddenly with great intensity and launches an attack before it even has a chance to ask, "Are you friend or foe?"

Before inquiring into the present state of scientific knowledge about sexual orientation, we had better ask scientists if they can tell us anything useful about anger. If we can't figure out how to deal with the anger that surges hot within us when we talk to each other in the church about sexuality, then listening to what scientists have to say about sexual orientation is likely to be nothing more than an exercise in looking for ammunition to use in a battle.

Many reviews of the scientific literature on sexual orientation have been compiled and published. What is most apparent in many of these reviews is that their authors have found data to shore up whatever case they already wanted to make. On the other hand, some authors have tried hard to write careful, balanced, and objective reviews of the scientific literature. Those authors have drawn hostile fire from both directions.

In Vietnam in 1968, the sound of incoming mortars and rockets was, to me, a signal that I should hunker down in the bottom of the nearest trench until the attack was over. We are in a situation in the church in which we need to be able to listen *empathetically* to one another and *critically* to scientists. In the present situation, *vigilant listening* will not serve well the life and mission of the church. But vigilant listening may be all that we are capable of if we envision our situation as a battlefield and see those who are otherwise-minded as particularly dangerous enemies.

Anger: A Word of Appreciation; a Word of Caution

Psychologists have been studying anger for decades now. Anger is an important and useful emotion. Anger focuses us and energizes us in situations in which narrow focus and high energy could spell the difference between life and death. One hates to think, for example, that there might be children in this world whose parents would not become focused and energized by anger when the well-being of their children is threatened.

Clearly we need to affirm the value of anger as a human emotion. A hard, angry edge to the voice is a useful way of signaling to others that we expect to be taken seriously. When we encounter a difficult obstacle on our way to an important goal, anger can keep us focused and energized when we might otherwise give up in discouragement.

But even as we affirm the value of anger as a human response, few of us are able to give unqualified endorsement to the nurturing and expressing of anger anymore. In the past decade we have seen too much road rage, too much air rage and desk rage, too many schoolyard shootings and workplace shootings, to be as innocent as we once were about nurturing anger within ourselves or venting anger freely toward others. It has been standard fare in self-help books that if we feel anger, we need to vent it lest we jeopardize our emotional health. This widespread cultural belief in the necessity of venting anger for the sake of our own mental health was parodied in the movie *Analyze This*, as cited later in *Personality and Social Psychology Bulletin*: "A psychiatrist (played by Billy Crystal) tells his New York gangster client (played by Robert DeNiro), 'You know what I do when

I'm angry? I hit a pillow. Try that.' The client promptly pulls out his gun, points it at the couch, and fires several bullets into the pillow. 'Feel better?' asks the psychiatrist. 'Yeah, I do,' says the gunman."[1]

All of the solid scientific research on the effects of venting anger has led to precisely the opposite conclusion: the most predictable outcome of venting anger, even at a pillow or a Wham-It doll, is that we become even angrier. Scientists have one other important reason for cautioning us against nurturing anger within and among ourselves: "Anxiety and anger increase vulnerability to illnesses, compromise the immune system, increase lipid levels, exacerbate pain, and increase the risk of death from cardiovascular disease and from all sources of death."[2]

Anger and Conflict:
Perspectives from the Bible and Science

Anger is a necessary emotion; anger is a dangerous emotion. Since anger animates many of the present discussions in churches about sexual orientation, we need a deeper understanding of what both the Bible and science have to say about the role of anger in human conflict. Anger is inevitable in the present discussions in our churches because important things are at stake. If there were no anger, it might just mean that we were trivializing important issues or regarding each other as people not worth taking seriously. But Jesus cautioned his disciples of serious dangers to watch for and avoid when anger surged among them. If they did not heed his caution, they were likely to become servants of their emotions, and their mission was likely to become a casualty of war.

In the Sermon on the Mount, Jesus offered his disciples acute insights into the functions of anger and fear in human community. It is important, as we talk together in the churches about emotionally charged issues, that we take with full seriousness what Jesus said about these powerful emotions. Perhaps current scientific research on anger and fear can help motivate us to listen more carefully to what our Lord had to say about these things.

Remember: The two basic functions of anger and fear are (1) to narrow down our focus to the present moment and (2) to give us an irresistible urge to act immediately.

Isaiah probably had a better understanding of these basic functions of anger and fear than we do today. Isaiah lived at a time and in a place where venturing out on the road made one vulnerable to ending up as dinner for a hungry lion (Isa. 35:9). When a lion sprang at you from the bushes that lined the road, you were less likely to survive if you weighed your alternatives, admired the beauty of the sunset, thought about being late for an appointment, worried about what your friends would think, considered the moral implications inherent in the situation, or pondered the likely consequences—even one minute into the future—

of any action that you might take. In the situation Isaiah alludes to, anger and fear offer one's best shot at survival for precisely the reason that I have just described: it narrows one's focus and impels one with an irresistible urge to act immediately.

In the Sermon on the Mount, Jesus warned of the dangers inherent in the very features of anger that make it so valuable. Today, anyone who doubts those real dangers might want to meet a mild-mannered businessman who is presently serving a prison term for a death that he caused during an episode of road rage. This man could tell you that any thoughts about the future pain that his action would bring to his children, or of the shame that his action will continue to bring to his grandchildren fifty years from now, were not accessible to his mind at a time when anger narrowed his focus and flooded him with a sense of urgency that he could not resist. The insult of that moment needed to be avenged at that moment! No other considerations were accessible to his mind at that instant. He now anticipates that he will weep over that for the rest of his life.

Concerning Anger's Forbidden Zone: The Sermon on the Mount

The Sermon on the Mount is a set of instructions for the conduct of our common life—our life together in community—as followers of Jesus. As a psychologist, I never cease to be amazed by the insights that this sermon offers into the dynamics of powerful human emotions such as anger, anxiety, and sexual desire. There is in this Sermon an unparalleled depth of understanding of the role these emotions play, for good or for ill, in human community.

Jesus noted that when people get angry at each other, they are likely to attach dismissive, degrading, and contemptuous labels to whoever evokes their anger. That is not something new, and it is not an American cultural invention. Jesus was well aware of a universal human temptation to attach dismissive, degrading, and contemptuous labels to others with whom we are in conflict, and he saw it as one of the things that he needed to caution his followers against in the strongest possible terms. If I may offer a paraphrase of Jesus' observations: "When heated disagreements arise among you, you will be tempted to say 'Raca!'[3] And when things get super-heated you will be tempted to say, 'You fool!' This, above all, is a temptation that you must resist!" (see Matt. 5:22).

Please note carefully the context in which Jesus anticipates that dismissive and contemptuous labels may become a problem: Jesus is not describing name-calling in the schoolyard, in the workplace, or on the street: he makes it abundantly clear that he is describing relationships within the community of faith, concerning which he has just noted, "You are the light of the world" (Matt. 5:14). This imagery of a community of faith providing light to the world is also found in Isaiah 58. There too it is the quality of their life together that makes their light shine forth. The people who bear God's name are called to relate to one another with hospitality, empathy, and compassion that transcend the normally defined limits of hospitality, empathy, and compassion: "Then shall your light break forth like the dawn" (Isa. 58:6-8).

And what happens when, within that same community of faith, people apply dismissive and contemptuous labels to those who evoke anger in them? "Raca! You fool!" Then the light dims and dies, and the community that was designated "light of the world" becomes the community that makes the name of God to be a laughingstock among the nations. Does that apply to our present situation? Again I will try to paraphrase the admonition of Jesus to his followers: "When you become angry at one another within the community of faith, you will not view one another with contempt, and you will not apply to one another dismissive labels."

As Lutherans we should not be surprised if we suddenly realize that we are most in need of confessing our sins precisely in those areas of life in which we are most firmly convinced of our own righteousness. Martin Luther wisely cautioned us to be suspicious of our own motives and alert to our own proclivities to self-deception. In our present discussions of sexuality, we seem to be creating our own variations on "Raca! You fool!" Please look carefully at the literature that has been disseminated in the churches by organizations on both sides of the controversy over homosexuality. Look especially carefully at the cartoons and caricatures. Listen carefully for the verbal caricatures that arise when the folks on either side of this issue get together to have lunch and gossip about the folks who take the opposite position.

It is particularly easy for Lutherans to convince ourselves that the Sermon on the Mount is irrelevant, "an impossible demand, intended to drive us to despair and into the arms of a Gracious Savior," and for that reason it need not be taken seriously by us at all. Has the notion that Jesus might have been serious when he said to his followers collectively, "You are the light of the world," come to seem merely preposterous to us? Have we so immersed ourselves in a culture of individualism that we quite automatically engage in some mental sleight-of-hand that makes it possible for us to read Jesus' words about the "light of the world" as if those words had nothing to do with our life together as a community but were merely a description of private virtues that we are to cultivate within ourselves as individual believers?

Anger is a useful emotion, but as followers of Jesus we venture into anger's forbidden zone when it motivates us to label others dismissively and contemptuously: "Raca! You fool!" As Christians we are in anger's forbidden zone when we say, concerning a brother or sister in Christ, "Faggot!" But are we not also in anger's forbidden zone when we say, concerning a brother or sister in Christ, "Heterosexist!"? We are in anger's forbidden zone not only when we say, "Queer!" but also when we say, "Homophobe!" Either way, we are using language to dismiss contemptuously the person being so labeled.

Listening to Luther about the Eighth Commandment

Martin Luther had some extremely important things to say with regard to carrying on our relationships within the community of disciples of Jesus. Two of Luther's insights are particularly relevant to us in our present discussion of homosexuality within our congregations. First, he advised us to maintain a healthy suspicion of our own motives, always being aware that we are vulnerable to distorting our perceptions in ways that are advantageous to ourselves at the expense of others. Second, he called on us to try to interpret the actions and motives of our sisters and brothers in Christ in the most favorable light we can.

In scientific research conducted during the past two decades, hundreds (maybe even thousands) of research projects have documented the accuracy of Luther's insights: there is a universal human tendency to distort reality in ways that make ourselves look good at the expense of making those who disagree with us look bad. It is a motive that operates below the level of conscious awareness. It is a motive about which Jesus had much to say: "Why do you see the speck in your neighbor's eye, but do not notice the log in your own eye? Or how can you say to your neighbor, 'Let me take the speck out of your eye,' while the log is in your own eye? You hypocrite, first take the log out of your own eye, and then you will see clearly to take the speck out of your neighbor's eye" (Matt. 7:3-4).

Some practical advice for people in conflict emerges from these biblical and theological insights. In conflicts, our thinking about the one with whom we are in conflict is likely to be influenced in two important ways. This has been amply documented by scientific research and is now being implemented in therapeutic approaches to the healing of relationships: We are likely to attribute the opinions, choices, and actions of others to *bad motives,* and we are likely to attribute the motives of others to *bad character.*

Marriage and family counselors are beginning to discover the usefulness of helping conflicted families to identify these patterns of distorted interpretation and to recognize the destructive role that they play in relationships.

In conflict, we are likely to attribute the other person's opinions and actions to bad motives:

Q: "Why do you think your kid does that?"
A: "He just wants to irritate me."

In conflict, we are likely to attribute the other person's motives to bad character:

Q: "Why would your kid want to irritate you?"
A: "He's just got a mean streak in him, that's all."

Watch the news reports about the culture wars. Notice how likely it is that people label those who see things differently than they do as having bad motives, or defective or even evil character. Look at the labels, for example, used by people on both sides of the capital punishment issue.

> Q: "Why do you think your neighbor favors capital punishment?"
> A: "He's basically a vengeful person."

> Q: "Why do you think your neighbor is opposed to capital punishment?"
> A: "He's just one of those 'bleeding heart' types."

Our conversations in the church over issues of sexuality would be well served, and so would our mission, if we were ever mindful of Luther's insights. We must monitor ourselves for a persistent tendency to interpret conflicts in ways that make ourselves look good while regarding the one who sees things differently as being moved by bad motives and having defective or evil character. And every time we catch ourselves doing that, we must repent.

The Relationship Killers: Contempt, Betrayal, and Exclusion

A lot of things make people angry, but they get over it quickly and their relationships are not seriously damaged. If you have been around children, you have probably noticed that they often get angry if they can't do what they want to do. A three-year-old who has been promised a family picnic can get pretty mad if it rains. A thirteen-year-old can become upset about being required to mow the lawn. These kinds of anger don't last very long, and growing up entails learning to deal with demands and disappointments without getting overly distressed. When people speak or act in ways that offend one another in these kinds of conflicts, the relationships can be easily healed, and it doesn't require the power of the Holy Spirit to make forgiveness possible.

Scientists have documented three kinds of experiences that are most likely to either crush the spirit of a human being or to produce anger that burns with intense and destructive heat and lasts for a long time—sometimes for generations or even centuries.[4] These are betrayal, contempt, and exclusion.

During the past decade, neuroscientists have been able to identify direct linkages between experiences of betrayal, contempt, and exclusion, and the areas in the brain that regulate aggression and depression.[5]

If you look at the schoolyard shootings, the workplace shootings, and the road-rage killings during the past couple of decades, all of them have been committed by people who perceived themselves as objects of betrayal, contempt, or exclusion. I could illustrate that point, but you can find plenty of examples of this for yourself in tomorrow's newspaper, whenever tomorrow happens to be. If understanding the power of betrayal, contempt, and exclusion in human life and human community is a key to understanding tomorrow's headlines, I believe it is also a key to understanding the gospel of Jesus Christ and the relevance of that gospel to conflict in the church.

The passion story of Jesus, as we read it in Matthew, Mark, and Luke, is a story of betrayal, contempt, and exclusion. We are likely to miss that point if we read the crucifixion story as if it were a story of physical agony. Entire books have been written about the physical pain involved in death by crucifixion, but the physical pain of Jesus is hardly noted at all in the Gospels. Here are the words that appear in the descriptions of the passion of Jesus according to Matthew, Mark, and Luke (New Revised Standard Version). In relation to Jesus, a remarkable variety of people are described as having

"derided him" (Matt. 27:39; Mark 15:29; Luke 23:39),
"scoffed at him" (Luke 23:35),
"mocked him" (Matt. 27:29, 31, 41; Mark 15:20, 31; Luke 22:63; 23:11, 36),
"spat on him" (Matt. 26:67; 27:30; Mark 14:65; 15:19; Luke 18:32),
"insulted him" (Luke 22:65),
"taunted him" (Matt. 27:44; Mark 15:32),
and "looked upon him with contempt" (Mark 9:12; Luke 23:11).

Is that utterly irrelevant to the present discussions about sexuality in our churches? People on each side of this issue seem quite willing to exclude those on the other side as not having valid concerns to bring to the table. People in this discussion are all too quick to regard a difference of opinion as a betrayal. People in this discussion are sometimes all too eager to turn away from each other in disgust or attack one another with moral indignation. Many people bring with them to these conversations strong expectations of betrayal by their leaders in the church. What is needed is this: people on each side of this issue must listen respectfully and acknowledge the full validity of the concerns that motivate those on the other side. People on each side of this issue must address seriously the concerns of those on the other side. People in leadership positions must speak directly and openly to the concerns of those who anticipate that the decisions have already been made and that they have already been betrayed. I will describe some of those concerns as voiced on both sides of the issue, and I will try to make a case for the validity of these concerns. In a conflict, both sides press for victory. Marriage counselors have a word of wisdom for us in this regard when they say to their clients, "You both want to win this conflict, but if either of you wins, the relationship loses."

To Both Sides:
A Resounding "Yes" and a Resounding "No"

The mission that our Lord has given us is at stake in our discussions of sexuality in the church, but not in the way that many people think. The mission of the church will not be advanced by victory for either side in the current controversy over homosexuality. It will not be advanced by victory for those who think that ordaining practicing homosexuals is a matter of social justice. Nor will it be advanced by victory for those who think that condemning homosexuality is a matter of taking the Bible seriously and maintaining social order in a time of widespread social chaos. The mission of the church will be furthered if the people on those two sides can talk and listen to each other without attacking in moral outrage or turning away in moral disgust. It will be furthered if they can listen empathetically and respectfully to those with whom they vigorously disagree and say to each other, "I can understand the legitimacy of the point you are trying to make, even if I don't agree with you on this issue. I will respond to your questions and concerns in a way that respects you as morally serious people of faith and that respects your questions as honest and serious questions. I will monitor myself for the sin of dismissing you with contempt."

Anger and disgust are powerful natural energizers. The moral outrage of those who see the homosexuality issue as one of social justice, and the moral disgust of those who see the homosexuality issue as one of maintaining social order and faithfulness to the Bible, hardly need to be augmented by "power from on high." It is extremely important that we pursue social justice, and it is extremely important that we seek social order. These are natural human motives that concern all people everywhere. They are important motives, but neither of them is the "narrow way" (Matt. 7:13) that Jesus describes in the Sermon on the Mount. Neither of them requires that we be "clothed with power from on high."[6]

Here are suggestions as to how each side could follow the "narrow way" that Jesus calls us to walk in our life together as people who bear his name in the world.

People who see this as a matter of social justice need to pause and acknowledge the validity of the following concerns: In many of its dimensions, the sexual revolution of the 1970s has done incalculable harm. It has resulted in a situation in which more than 40 percent of this nation's ninth graders have already had sexual intercourse, many with multiple partners.[7] It has undermined the stability of families. It has promoted promiscuity. It is one of many factors that have contributed to tripling the suicide rate among American teenagers during the past thirty years. It has crushed the spirits of millions of people. It has contributed to a situation in which our children learn about their sexuality by watching pornography on the Internet (it is estimated that one-third of Internet users visit pornography sites.) When people say that none of these things has been good for our children or for our society, they are right. When they say that the movement for gay rights coincides in time with the sexual revolution that has been so disastrous in so many ways, they are right. When they ask why gay-rights activism should not be seen as just one more dimension of the sexual chaos that has done so much damage, they deserve to be regarded as serious people who are asking serious questions that deserve serious answers. They do not deserve to be dismissively labeled as "right-wing extremists," no matter how satisfying those labels may feel to those who apply them to others. They do not deserve to be seen as people motivated by bad motives and bad character. We sin against them when we dismiss them as promoters of injustice and attack them (from a safe distance) in moral outrage. We must listen to their concerns and questions as the honest concerns and legitimate questions of serious people.

At the same time, people who see this as an issue of social order and faithfulness to the Bible also have taken the broad and easy road. They have labeled both homosexuals and their advocates as disgusting and have regarded their opinions as rooted in bad motives and bad character. They need to take seriously the fact that there are at least some data that suggest that sexual orientation may be heavily influenced by factors at work before an individual is born. In twin studies, if one identical twin is gay, the likelihood that the other one will be gay is about fifty percent. While these data are open to interpretation, they may well indicate that prenatal factors powerfully influence or even determine the development of sexual orientation. More importantly, almost all gay and lesbian people say that their own experience was not that they "chose a gay lifestyle" but that they became aware of their "sexual orientation" in the same way and at about the same developmental stage when heterosexual adolescents become aware of their "sexual orientation." People who look at this information often assert: "If sexual orientation is not a matter of individual choice, then it is an issue of justice that is at stake when we discuss whether homosexual persons should receive church blessings for their relationships or be eligible for ordained service in the church." People who ask these questions ask them in all seriousness. They must be listened to, respected, and responded to as morally serious people when they say, "We see this is an issue of justice." In our congregations, those who have applied pejorative and dismissive labels to those who see this as an issue of justice must scrutinize themselves in the light of the Eighth Commandment.

The Context in Which We Listen to Experience

As Christians we listen attentively, respectfully, and empathetically to one another's experience. We do so because we know ourselves as a community that has been commissioned by our Lord as stewards of his mission. We do not listen as members of a community of like-minded people, ever vigilant to exclude or betray or condemn the otherwise-minded. The context in which we listen to one another is that of a people whose life together is constituted by our baptism into the death and resurrection, the community and mission of Jesus. That's not a sentimental story of sweetness and light; it's a task so hard that we are cautioned by our Lord that it will require being "clothed with power from on high." To turn away in disgust or attack in moral outrage—*that* would be the easy way out.

Listening to Scientists about Sexual Orientation

Dear Ann Landers: I recently found out that my 22-year-old brother is gay. I am in a total state of shock. He has told only me and my older sister, and we are both confused about how to handle it.

—Alabama

Dear Alabama: Your brother did not decide to become gay. He was born that way. I hope all the family members will accept the situation. His sexual orientation does not change the kind of person he is. . . .[8]

Ann Landers was one of many figures in the popular media who have confidently proclaimed in recent years that scientists have already said the definitive word about sexual orientation. "There's a gene for it" is the way many people state what they believe to be an "established scientific fact." People who believe this to be the current state of scientific knowledge also generally are convinced that moral decision-making is intuitively and immediately obvious on the basis of their information. As one man said in a church meeting that I attended, "If you want to know what causes sexual orientation, ask a geneticist." That's an interesting assertion for many reasons, as we will see. However, had this man actually consulted a geneticist, he might have discovered that the situation is a bit more complex than he believed it to be. That complexity might have tempered his opinion about of church members who disagreed with him.

The research on sexual orientation that was published through the end of the twentieth century has been summarized and reviewed in more than a dozen articles and several books. I have read many of those articles and books as well as many reviews written in response to them. Some of the articles' and books' authors are clear partisans on one side or the other of the conflict over homosexuality, while others try hard to take a balanced and impartial look at the research. Without exception these authors have been both praised and vilified by reviewers. An author who undertakes to write about the present state of scientific knowledge regarding sexual orientation invites praise from those who believe that they have been provided with powerful weapons, and condemnation from those who see the author as collaborating with the enemy. Much of this reaction is rooted in a serious misunderstanding of what science is, and a failure to appreciate the complexity of scientific research into human sexuality in general and sexual orientation in particular. Listening to the debate about sexual orientation in the churches from the perspective of a behavioral scientist, I am troubled by the misuse of scientific research data by partisans on both sides of this debate.

I decided to look at what has been published since the turn of the new millennium. Between January 2000 and June 2002, more than six hundred research articles about sexual orientation were published in scientific journals of biology, neuroscience, psychology, and the social sciences. As of June 2002, scientists do not yet have definitive answers to the questions that people are asking about sexual orientation—but it isn't for lack of trying.

What Do Scientists Know about Sexual Orientation? What Do We Want Them to Tell Us?

Scientists are looking at sexual orientation from a wide variety of perspectives. No framework for classifying the research can include it all, but it appears that the following five categories are attracting the most interest from researchers:

Cause: What "causes" sexual orientation?

Change: Can sexual orientation be changed?

Attitudes: How can attitudes toward homosexuality be measured? How do these attitudes develop? Are these attitudes presently changing among the general public?

Mental health: Are significant mental health issues (e.g., loneliness, depression, suicide) associated with sexual orientation? What is the nature of the association? What should mental health workers be mindful of to effectively serve gay and lesbian clients?

Parenting: Is child development affected by being raised by two same-sex parents?

My next point may disappoint many readers, but it happens to be true: The things we are most eager to learn about are the very things scientists have the hardest time studying and can tell us least about. The question that comes up first in every discussion is "What causes it?" In virtually every summary of the scientific research about sexual orientation, the first section of the book or article is devoted to the question "What causes it?" We will address that question in a moment.

But what about the other questions: Can sexual orientation be changed? Can two same-sex parents raise children effectively? Neither of those questions has yet generated research that can be regarded as scientifically respectable. Even under the most carefully controlled research conditions, human motives can skew the data and distort the outcomes of the research projects. With regard to both of these questions, the research outcomes must be attributed primarily to the motivations of the researchers and the research subjects.

With regard to mental health issues, there are so many variables influencing the data that anybody can make as valid an interpretation as anybody else. If someone wants to interpret mental health statistics among a population of gay or lesbian people as reflecting something about their sexual orientation, others could, with equal validity, interpret these same statistics as being the outcome of stigmatization.

With regard to the question of attitude change, here we find the only clear data that scientific studies of sexual orientation have produced. If public-opinion polling is a science, it is one of the most straightforward sciences, and the results seem straightforward: The American public has shifted greatly toward a more favorable view of homosexual persons during the past decade. But even though the data are unambiguous, the interpretation of those data are not. I asked numerous people about their own attitudes toward issues of sexual orientation and whether their attitudes had changed. I also presented numerous people with statistics on this shift toward a more favorable attitude. My respondents had evenly divided opinions on this. Some said, "It's due to positive presentations of homosexual persons in the popular media." Others said with equal certainty, "It's because people we know and love have let us know that they were homosexual, and they didn't stop being the same wonderful people that we had always known and loved." Who is right about this? Your opinion is probably as valid as anyone else's.

Do Scientists Know
What Causes Sexual Orientation?

Contrary to much popular opinion, a "gay gene" has not been identified at this time. Most geneticists now believe that when causality is finally determined, it will be much more complex than the identification of a single genetic factor. It is difficult to convey the complexity of the research task that scientists are faced with in trying to identify causal factors related to homosexuality, and I think that the only way I can do that is to describe a particular ongoing research project. This may try your patience, but I invite you to stay with me for a paragraph or two.

Those who believe that the task of identifying a biological basis for homosexuality is simple and straightforward should try reading some of the research now being published. They may find themselves floundering around in articles about "dermatoglyphic directional asymmetry and sexual orientation."[9] I cite this line of research not because of the obscurity of the language but because it demonstrates the kind of indirectness that is presently required in scientific investigations into the origins of sexual orientation.

The reasoning behind this research goes like this: Whether one is right- or left-handed is not a matter of choice; neither can one choose one's fingerprints. If homosexuality can be demonstrated to correlate with handedness or with some atypical characteristic of fingerprints, that might "support . . . a biological basis of sexual orientation." Earlier research had reported an association in men between homosexuality and the fingerprint characteristic called "dermatoglyphic directional asymmetry." Earlier research had also reported an association in women between non-right-handedness and homosexual orientation. This research project was attempting to replicate and extend the earlier findings. The study was not conclusive, and the associations were not robust, but the authors felt that their results did lend support to "a biological basis of sexual orientation."

I really hesitate to describe this kind of research, because even among scientists it is not easy for nonspecialists to follow. Yet if we are to be realistic about the present state of scientific knowledge about the causes of sexual orientation, both sides of the debate need to hear the implications of this kind of study. People who argue that "science knows" exactly what causes sexual orientation need to acknowledge that if scientists *really* had identified a gene for sexual orientation, respected researchers who want to establish "a biological basis for sexual orientation" would not be investing this kind of energy, time, and money trying to establish a biological link through such indirect research.

On the other hand, people who argue that sexual orientation is a "lifestyle choice" need to acknowledge the possibility that the kind of research described above may actually succeed some day in identifying a precise set of biological conditions for the emergence of the sexuality of homosexual, heterosexual, and transgendered individuals. In the meantime, dogmatic statements about what "science knows" about the origins of sexual orientation are simply wrong.

Scientists presently do not know what causes sexual orientation, but they are trying hard to find out, pursuing such questions as:

- Does sexual orientation have a genetic basis?
- Is sexual orientation related to maternal hormonal levels during gestation?
- Is sexual orientation correlated with birth order in males?
- Is sexual orientation a "cultural invention"?
- Is sexual orientation influenced by the interaction of some or all of these factors?

Why Is It So Important to Know What Causes Sexual Orientation?

In most of the discussions about sexual orientation that I have participated in, at some point someone has angrily asked, "What difference does it make what the causes are? We shouldn't be asking that question!" Well, whether we ought to be asking that question or not, we are asking it, and we will continue to ask it. It is fundamental to our human nature to seek to make sense of our experience, and one of the most basic ways in which people everywhere try to make sense of events that are important to them, or phenomena that perplex them, is by asking the question "What causes it?"

Science itself has its origins in that question. Here are some examples: When Galileo observed events in the heavens, he asked, "What causes that?" and proceeded systematically to seek answers to his questions. Many of us can expect to live longer, healthier lives than our ancestors did because medical scientists are always asking, "What causes that?" and systematically seeking answers. Half a century ago parents in many places worried—all summer, every summer—that their children might get a disabling and often fatal disease called polio. The first step toward ending that epidemic was to seek an answer to the question "What causes it?" Psychologists have noted that some individuals can thrive in the face of adverse situations that are emotionally damaging to most people. They have asked, "What causes that?" and have learned things that can help us all cope more effectively with the stresses of our lives. Scientists will continue to ask the question "What causes it?"

Nonscientists too will continue to think about events in terms of their causes. How we react to important events and people will be shaped, or even determined, by the way we answer the question "What caused it?" As I write these words, I am sitting in a crowded airport waiting to catch a plane from Chicago to Kansas City. Suddenly, from behind, someone lurches heavily into my left shoulder. My notebook computer almost slides from my lap. I feel a surge of anger as the thought "Clumsy oaf!" comes into my mind. I turn around. A harried young mother is trying to manage three tired, restless little boys. She is crying. "I'm so sorry," she sobs. In an instant my anger gives way to compassion. "You've got a tough job there," I reply. "Is there anything I can do to help?"

Like us, the disciples of Jesus also asked the question. When the Twelve encountered events that perplexed, bewildered, or threatened them, that called into question the orderliness and predictability of their world and threatened their sense of safety, they asked, "What causes it?" One day when Jesus happened upon a man who had been born blind, his disciples asked him, "Rabbi, who sinned, this man or his parents, that he was born blind?" (John 9:1-2). Please note: they asked Jesus a multiple-choice question, assuming there were only two valid answers that would restore to them a sense that their world was an orderly, reliable, predictable place and that they were safe in it. All of that was threatened by the reality of a man who was born blind. If our world is a place in which a person can be born blind, how can we live in it with a sense of safety and trust? We can do that quite easily if we attribute this tragic event to either of two causes: his sin or the sin of his parents. It is that approach to the question of causality that Jesus rules "out of bounds" for those who are called to follow him.

Curiosity is not the only motive that leads humans to ask the question "What causes it?" Nor is a desire for truth the only motive that guides our search for an answer. When the disciples of Jesus asked, "Rabbi, who sinned, this man or his parents, that he was born blind?" neither the question nor the answers that they would entertain as valid were motivated by a desire to know the truth. The reliability and predictability of their world and their own desire to regard themselves as both safe and good people were what was at stake.

Today, a large body of very good scientific research documents that those are often the motives that impel all human beings, ourselves included, to ask the question "What causes it?"[10] It is a self-serving motive that operates below the level of conscious awareness, aimed at providing us with a sense of our own goodness and safety at the expense of viewing others as bad people who deserve whatever evil may befall them. As Lutherans we ought not to be surprised to find such motives lurking behind the disguise of "noble scientific" questions that we might ask. As followers of Jesus, we know that such self-justification is a denial of the gospel and that finding safety in such "cognitive distortions" is an abandonment of faith. The word "faith" is used in several ways in the Bible. In Matthew's Gospel, whenever the word "faith" refers to those who follow Jesus as disciples, it always indicates the call to surrender their own efforts at safety and to trust in their Lord: "And when he got into the boat, his disciples followed him. A windstorm arose on the sea, so great that the boat was being swamped by the waves . . ."(Matt. 8:23-24). When Jesus said to his disciples in that situation, "Why are you afraid, you of little faith?" perhaps he was also speaking to us in our present situation. Perhaps he was reminding us that faithful discipleship today still means following Jesus into stormy places—even into the storms of controversy that presently characterize the discussions about homosexuality. Perhaps Jesus was reminding us too that following him faithfully requires that we transcend considerations of our own safety and goodness and conduct ourselves amid the storm as people whose lives and relationships are directed and empowered by faith in Jesus.

Discussion Questions

1. This chapter makes a distinction between empathetic listening and vigilant listening. Is empathetic listening possible when the issues we are discussing

evoke such strong feelings? Does our understanding of life together in Christ help us?

2. How might Jesus' call to practice humility apply when hotly contested issues are under discussion? Does the practice of humility prevent us from taking a strong stand for our convictions?

3. How important is it that we know more about the causes of homosexuality? Can more scientific knowledge resolve disputes over the acceptability of homosexual behavior?

4. How do you understand the mission of your congregation in your larger community? What role does the present discussion of sexuality play in that mission?

For Further Reading

Bellis, Alice Ogden, and Terry L. Hufford. *Science, Scripture, and Homosexuality.* Cleveland: Pilgrim Press, 2002.

Gudorf, Christine E. "The Bible and Science on Sexuality." *Homosexuality, Science, and the "Plain Sense" of Scripture.* Ed. David L. Balch. Grand Rapids: Eerdmans, 2000.

Jones, Stanton L., and Mark A. Yarhouse. "The Use, Misuse, and Abuse of Science in the Ecclesiastical Homosexuality Debates." *Homosexuality, Science, and the "Plain Sense" of Scripture.* Edited by David L. Balch. Grand Rapids: Eerdmans, 2000.

Strommen, Merton P. *The Church and Homosexuality: Searching for a Middle Ground.* Revised edition. Minneapolis: Kirk House Publishers, 2002.

Notes

1. Brad Bushman, "Venting Anger Feeds the Flame," *Personality and Social Psychology Bulletin,* June 2002.

2. Richard M. Suinn, "The Terrible Twos—Anger and Anxiety: Hazardous to Your Health" *American Psychologist,* January 2001.

3. "An obscure term of abuse," according to the Oxford annotated edition of the New Revised Standard Version.

4. If you inquire about the campaigns of "ethnic cleansing" in eastern Europe in the past decade, you will hear stories of betrayal and humiliation that date back more than eight hundred years.

5. See, for example, Eddie Harmon-Jones and Jonathan Sigelman, "State anger and prefrontal brain activity: Evidence that insult-related relative left-prefrontal activation is associated with experienced anger and aggression." *Journal of Personality and Social Psychology,* May 2001.

6. Please note: Jesus is not describing the "narrow way" of morally heroic individuals in this passage; he is describing the "narrow way" of a community life that differs from the way people ordinarily live their lives together in community.

7. Statistic from the Centers for Disease Control and Prevention as reported by David G. Myers, *The American Paradox: Spiritual Hunger in an Age of Plenty* (New Haven, Yale University Press, 2000).

8. *Telegraph Herald,* Dubuque, Iowa, April 18, 2002.

9. Brian Mustanski, Michael Bailey, and Sarah Kaspar, "Dermatoglyphics, Handedness, Sex, and Sexual Orientation," *Archives of Sexual Behavior,* February 2002.

10. Carolyn L. Hafer, "Do Innocent Victims Threaten the Belief in a Just World?" *Journal of Personality and Social Psychology,* August 2000.

Authors' Forum

May 29, 2002

JMC: James M. Childs Jr.
JN: James Arne Nestingen
DO: Daniel L. Olson
RP: Richard J. Perry Jr.
MAP: Mark Allan Powell
JDR: José David Rodríguez
MS: Martha Ellen Stortz

What do you believe is the importance of this book?

MAP: I think a study like this is important because there is concern within our church as to whether our church policies are best in keeping with the will of God as understood in the light of Holy Scripture. There are many within our church that are questioning whether the church's attitudes, policies, and practices regarding gay and lesbian people are those that God would want us to have. So it is important for leaders in the church to examine the Scriptures and traditions and to think theologically about these issues and to explore together what we believe God might be saying to us at this time.

JDR: One important thing is try to realize that between extremes there are always opportunities to see creative and thoughtful appropriation of tradition. We need to carefully discern not what is being stereotyped but what is being taught by significant partners that need to be in this conversation. The opportunity to be open to other positions, without giving up what one thinks, is what enables one to be able to be faithful and to do it in a spirit of collaboration.

DO: To me this is an important project because I think this is a genuine crisis for the church in the technical meaning of the term "crisis" in the Greek language. It means a situation out of which you cannot emerge the same as you went in. You can either come out weaker or stronger, better or worse, more whole or more fragmented, more or less faithful. I think that this is a situation in which we will either come out stronger or weaker. I hope that this project will contribute to us being able to discuss these issues as congregations and as synods and as a church in such a way that we demonstrate to ourselves that we can be faithful even though we are dealing with really hot-button issues, issues that have a lot of emotion attached to them and on which we strongly differ in our opinions. I think that is what the world needs from us now. As the world becomes more and more fragmented, it needs a demonstration that it is possible to find unity that is not based simply on like-mindedness or shared experience, but that we find a unity that is ours in our baptismal identity.

RP: I think that this project is important because I think in today's world there is a need to continue to provide resources that can assist congregations to experience what it means to have a conversation and a dialogue about issues and concerns that are controversial. My hope is that this project will, through various chapters, give pastors and congregations some material to reflect upon and also to have material that they can to talk to each other about. And I hope that they will experience, through our own conversation and dialogue with the various chapters, a sense of hope that all is not lost but that there is a sense of hope that as Christians we can dialogue together in a very civil manner.

JN: I think that this volume is important for a couple of reasons. First of all, Carl Barth once said that daily witness begins with the Scripture in one hand and the daily newspaper in the other. In the issues of sexuality the daily newspaper has a way of taking over and setting a standard exclusively, making it very difficult for the church to register a biblical word, a traditional word, a gospel word. In our conversation we have attempted to strike that balance. Secondly, we do not all agree, as will become evident in the course of this reading. We have differences among us as a group of writers. We have worked together quite closely, read each other's material, examined it, discussed it, learned from one another, and our conversation has been productive. We hope to be able to pass on to the church something of a model for a conversation that is faithful, not boring; provocative, spicy, engaging—and yet honoring our differences.

MS: I would say that this conversation, this book, is twofold, really. In it we have tried to offer a critical appropriation of some of the elements of a faithful conversation in terms of Scripture, the confessional witness, oral theology, cultural criticism, pastoral care and counseling. We have tried to offer elements of a faithful conversation but—and I think this is equally important—we have tried to offer it as an exercise in faithful conversation. To be a theologian in this church at the beginning of the twenty-first century is to already be out on this issue. We have written in many different venues on this issue; our positions are known both to members of the church and to one another; and how can we continue talking about this issue in a way that moves past stalemated, already-thought-through positions? My experience in this project is that we have each learned from one another, respected one another's positions, and come out in a different place than where we were when we entered. And I think if we can do that as a group of people who have thought a great deal about this, then we are offering this as a microcosm of faithful conversation as well—and that gives me great hope and pride and zeal.

JMC: I am currently serving as director for the ELCA Studies on Sexuality. I want to echo the comments of my colleagues regarding the modeling of dialogue in the church that this volume represents, and the rich interchange that we have enjoyed as we have edified one another in the process. I want to say a word or two about the significance of the book as a seminary product. While this volume is written by seminary professors of our ELCA schools, it does not have a representative from every seminary or from every conceivable point of view. It is nonetheless a good representation of the kind of scholarship that we have present among us in our seminaries, and it signals the fact that while everybody has an important role in the whole discussion, seminaries have a particular role and responsibility. Seminaries are preparing the leadership of the church and shaping the vision of those leaders and their theology and practice. They have this special role to play and therefore a special accountability to the church. In some ways this is one small expression of attempting to fulfill the duties of accountability to the church, by trying to take up this conversation in a way that will be edifying and will demonstrate faithfulness among the teachers of the church. I think those are thoughts that are important in thinking about this volume.

How might some of the folks in the church utilize this resource in the most helpful way?

JN: I can think of a couple of ways in which this study can be used. First of all, I am really concerned with some of the dimensions, issues, statements that, in discussion, tend to be like the abortion debate—with competing bumper stickers rather than conversation. And for that reason especially I have found among pastors some hesitance to really engage the issue, and I have been quite disappointed in that. I hope that one use of the work might be for pastors' text study groups to take on the issue together. I think a second use for it would be for pastors' congregations to work together on the issue, to talk it through together, to engage in differences. Thirdly, I think that there are a lot of Bible study groups that could pick up a volume like this. I have found a lot of really solid biblical sophistication and knowledge of the catechism in the church. There are people that would really enjoy entering the issue at a level where it is not cut and dried. This is *not* cut and dried. This is a conversation that has begun and invites continuation of such things.

MS: What I think is helpful about the way the conversation has been framed is that it does begin from different things that Christians hold in common. Certainly we all have sexual orientation. But the volume also expresses other commonalities. For instance, we come out of a culture. We are deeply cultured beings. We come out of a tradition of confessional tradition, a rich, lively, confessional tradition. This is something we share. What are the riches in that that can frame the conversation? We all know anger and fear, particularly around this issue. How can we access that as something that we all hold in common as we engage in these difficult decisions? We are all baptized Christians. How can that frame a new conversation about this? We all wrestle with the Scripture. How can that help us shape a new conversation? So I think that this volume really tries to play from those commonalities that every Christian has, as he or she gets to these sorts of positions. And I think that is helpful; it may even be fresh and new.

RP: I think, Marty, that you stirred in me something that I hope shows in the essay that José and I authored and that is that this can be a resource to help people in a truthful, faithful, and honest way to name what the sources of our involvement are in this particular issue. Sometimes I fear too much is kept behind the back or under the table. I have come to the conclusion that if we get into the public arena what the problems really are, we might be able to move a step or two in the conversation. Is it our confessional tradition? Is it our understanding of the Bible? Is it our understanding and interpretation of culture? Is it the anger we feel? I think we need to be able to name some things as they really are and not try to smooth it over. I think people are strong enough to be able to name things and talk to each other about it. I hope that this resource can help people to name what the issues are for themselves and for them to own them.

JDR: Maybe one of the disciplines that we have established is how we can deal with differences in the way that can help us each to reconstruct what we bring as our part of the whole, and not just to bring what we have as a weapon to challenge some other position as inadequate. And I think that is the discipline of thinking about ourselves connected to a community of moral deliberation that tries seriously to be a community and not just individual fragments fighting for one's ground at the cost of others.

MAP: I hope that the book will be used to further dialogue rather than just debate. On this difficult and controversial issue I think that we need to move beyond trying to shore up our own arguments and opinions and try earnestly to understand the opinions and positions of others. I do not have to accept your argument, but if you are my sister or brother in Christ, I must accept you and I want to understand your argument in a way that will help me to accept you and have fellowship with you as part of the community. It really seems to me that this book aids in that process. Dan Olsen says in his chapter that the church is not called to be a community of the like-minded; communities of the like-minded are easy to come by, and one does not need to be "clothed with power from on high" to be that. The power of the Holy Spirit enables us to be much more than a community of the like-minded. Marty Stortz says in her article that our primary orientation is given to us in baptism and our primary lifestyle is the lifestyle of discipleship. This book is for people who love Jesus Christ, for people who believe the Bible, for people who trust the Holy Spirit to work in the church through them and through their brothers and sisters, that we might all come to deeper appreciation and understanding of each other.

DO: I hope that this book will be a really practical help in the sense of providing some structure and safety for congregations that have to talk about something they may well wish they did not have to talk about. In my offices as pastoral care professor, I often get telephone calls from somebody saying they *have* to do something, and they wish they did not. They ask me, for example, how to tell their child that his mom has died. And there is no way out of it and it does not feel very safe. I think maybe we have arrived a point where there is no way out of it and it does not feel very safe. I hope that structuring some of these hard conversations around chapters in this book can provide a sense of safety—not to be found in simply sounding off what you are feeling, but rather some safety in taking a look at materials that have been carefully prepared by some thoughtful people who have done a lot of thinking about this.

JN: The issue of contexualism is very interesting because what we do not always see is that observing we *are* in a context is, itself, a contextual comment. And it shows particularly in this question; this is very much a North American question and to some extent a European question, though to a much lesser degree. Why is it that North Americans are asking this question? And why is it that churches that come from the upper middle class are asking this question? When I was in Tanzania several years ago, I had the opportunity to spend some time with the Maasai people, and they were very curious about why the North Americans are discussing this issue and couldn't quite figure it out. The fact that what has been ecumenically held in a consensus for two thousand years is all of a sudden unraveling before our eyes. The fact that we are now raising an issue that has not been a question maybe indicates something about ourselves that we need to think about quite closely, and reflect on, as we go to the biblical word, as we go to the Confessions, and as we go through the various traditions that are present in our community.

RP: Could this be because in North America the issue has evolved to a point where the debate in the public arena is now centered on rights? And that our culture, generally speaking, is convinced that, whatever may be my condition, it entitles me to certain rights? Therefore, because I feel I am entitled certain rights in society, the church, which has been a long-time advocate for the rights of people, will certainly be on my side when I claim my rights as who and what I am in the public arena. This is why we are facing this issue publicly, where before it had been very much a private matter. And so now we are asked to make policy statements, and people want to see the church make a policy statement, or want government to make laws that would sanction my definition of myself. This would not be a big issue on the continent of Africa.

JMC: I think you are on to something. Jim Nestingen used the *Roe v. Wade* Supreme Court decision as one example of the individualism of our society. One might argue that the court's decision reflects a postmodern secularity, which acknowledges no prevailing ethos, no prevailing worldview, no prevailing philosophical or religious framework, and, consequently, leaves moral conviction to the realm of privacy and individual choice. It is a situation in which communal values decidedly come in second. However, it is important to say that those in the church who want to stand fast with what we have taught and those who want to change and allow for the recognition of gay and lesbian unions are both not simply individualistic in their approach. The latter do want to say that persons in same-sex relationships are accountable, as are persons in heterosexual relationships.

DO: I think there are a number of factors that come together that have forced this issue to the forefront. In the last thirty years I think my field in psychology has contributed a lot of harm. I think about thirty or thirty-five years ago the idea was put in place in our society that the only value base is your own fulfillment and the maximization of your own experience. I think that is where a lot of fragmentation in our society has come from. I think this whole notion that my ultimate obligation is to the maximization of my own experience, and that all other commitments are secondary, is the source of a lot of the conflict in our society. If there is a conflict between my commitment to the maximization of my own experience and any other commitment that I have made, then that other commitment has got to go.

JN: *(responding in agreement)* "Only go around once in life, so you have got to grab for all the gusto you can get."

DO: It is amazing how many outfits are using as an advertising slogan "You deserve" or "Because you are worth it." It is also amazing how many companies use as an advertising strategy an appeal to some form of taking control.

JN: In a context like that, sexuality becomes commodified. It becomes mythologized. It becomes something that I can consume and experience. It gets mythologized in that expectations get inflated as though this is the experience beyond all experiences. And then people live with massive levels of disappointment and resentment, regret, sorrow. It becomes a demonic circle; "He who seeks his life will lose it, whoever loses his life for my sake will find it." The attempt to attain the self finally destroys it.

MS: And I think to the degree that this language of commodification and entitlement and rights has moved into the realm of Christian moral discourse, it has really impoverished the language of discipleship. I want to reassert the rich, thick notion of discipleship as a way of understanding Christian sexuality other than letting it be totally catalogued as another commodity. I think this volume and many of the essays in the volume are trying to reassert that rich language of discipleship.

DO: The problem with the commodification of sex is that it leads to the objectification of the other. I have heard theologians talk about lust as if it were synonymous with sexual feelings, but Erik Erikson gave us a better interpretation of lusting. He puts it in opposition to love. He says love is relating to the other as a subject, and lust turns the other into an object for gratification of desire. I talk about there being basic causes of the kind of anger that burns deep, hot, and lasts forever. One of them is contempt. Everyone knows intuitively that to be objectified is to be treated with contempt. To be turned into an object for the gratification of somebody else's desires is not to be a person any longer but to be a thing.

MS: It makes the language of the neighbor come forward with a new urgency. The neighbor, not the object, not the vehicle for my self-gratification. That language of the neighbor is really revolutionary language. I think we really want to present that boldly and without apology.

RP: Is not our tradition a living tradition? Is there not a living dynamic to the confessional tradition and our biblical tradition so that once we have been taught what certain passages mean it stays with you? It stayed with me for forty-five years. Now the church and culture are telling me something different, and it is creating some anger in me, and I want to strike out at the church and the preacher and say, "She/he must have been lying all along." That's understandable. But the larger the point that José and I want to make is that when we encounter other cultures, we encounter the possibility that the tradition we have learned and cherished could be changed in certain ways. So while we do have a deposit of the Christian faith that is for all times, a living tradition in that sense, it does not stay stagnant. It does change in encounter as we have more experiences with people, different experiences with people.

JN: Oftentimes the terms *multiculturalism* and *context* are used to thin down the soup. That is, to thin out what is rich and to reduce the specifics of it, to abstract it. As Jesse Jackson said, genuine multiculturalism is vegetable soup where each ingredient retains its particular flavor; then as it thickens it gains in flavor. It gets delicious because there are the contrasting flavors and they are each specific enough to flavor one another.

JDR: An important purpose of this book is to show that we should not withdraw from the challenges that we are confronted with but should address them with the vision of the good news of God. My concern is that there is a tendency, given our fallen nature, to see whatever challenge we confront as something we have to address in a confronting fashion. I guess in issues like homosexuality my concern is, how can I deal with such a provocative, conflictive, and difficult matter with a visional hope? I think that, for me, my faith tells me that I can do this, and it is an opportunity to test what I believe and a challenge to grow in faith. I think a project like this forces us to this kind of opportunity.

JMC: I think the importance of what you are saying has to do with the quality of the process that we go through as a church body in this whole business of making decisions. We are going to make some decisions. Even if we stand fast, that is a decision. If we make changes, that is a decision. If we frame a proposal that nobody has thought of yet, that is a decision. It is inescapable. The way in which we work with one another on the way to the time of decision will make all the difference in the world as to how we can deal with it once it happens. Predictably, not everybody is going to be uniformly happy with whatever the church finally does. The decision in 2005 may be just the first of a number of decisions that lie down the road. It will doubtless be a milestone, but not the end of the road. The way in which we travel together to that point will make a lot of difference as to what happens when we get there. I think that is where all the talk we have done about modeling and dialogue has its importance for the church.

DO: One of the passages in these manuscripts that really caught my attention and held it and moved me was the point in Marty's manuscript where she talks about promise-making and promise-keeping and its essential role in community. I find myself being asked by some people if the church is not saying today what it was saying twenty-five years ago when I came on board; is the church keeping its promise to me or am I being betrayed? And if I am being betrayed should not I abandon ship? I think about it and here is where I come down. Jesus talks about a householder who was going on a journey and called together the slaves and literally, in Greek, gave them *exousia,* gave them authority. "Put them in charge" is the translation. Now, he did not call them together and appoint them to be security guards at a warehouse. The function of somebody who has authority is to make decisions. The only reason that you would need a steward would be if there were going to be new situations that had come up that had never come up before, and somebody needed to make a decision about them. Otherwise, you just go by the rules. But he did not call them together and give them a set of rules. He called them together and gave them authority, and that means the authority to make new responses to new situations and make new choices when the world changes, when the context requires. I think that there is a sense that stewardship requires that we think through hard stuff and make choices.

What do we say to people who believe that we should not be doing this study at all? The church's teaching has been clear about this for as long as anybody can remember or record. Therefore, why should we be talking about it at all?

MAP: People may say that for different reasons. The reason I usually hear for why the church need not do a study on homosexuality is that people think what the Bible says is so absolutely clear, and the application and relevance of what the Bible says is so obvious, that there is no need for the church to consider it beyond that. However, there is virtually no biblical scholar of any persuasion who would agree that the Bible is absolutely clear and that matters of application and relevance are obvious. Almost any biblical scholar who has studied the Bible on this will admit, "This is what I think the Bible says we should do; I can understand why people might think otherwise." So I think that there *is* a perception out there in the church questioning why the church needs to study this; why can't we just do what the Bible says? On another level, when I hear somebody say that the church does not need to do a study like this, what they are saying is that I do not care about my brothers and sisters in Christ. I know what I believe and realize that many of my brothers and sisters in Christ do not agree with me, but I do not care enough about them to want to find out why they think the way they do, or to want to be in fellowship with them. That is what I hear behind that question.

DO: A few weeks ago *Newsweek* had a cover story on Christianity and Islam, and the author of that article was insightful enough to remark that the notion that the Bible is to the church what the Koran is to Islam is mistaken. The author of the article said *Jesus* is to the church as the Koran is to Islam. And I think we need to remember and teach that as the nature of our understanding of the Scripture. We, as Lutherans, perhaps need to remind ourselves from time to time that Luther said that the Bible is the manger in which Jesus was laid. We do not interact with the Bible as merely a repository of timeless propositions of theology and ethics but as the avenue of our encounter with a living God.

RP: Some people think that the church has already made up its mind on the issue. We just need to go ahead and decide and act, and not waste the resources and time studying what we already know we are going to do. A study is just a way of postponing or delaying. I have heard that opinion voiced on all sides of the debate.

MAP: I feel like I must really be out of the loop because I still do not know for sure what I believe about this—and if the church has supposedly already decided something and has its mind made up, I wonder how come nobody has brought me in on it.

DO: I think the perception that Richard named *needs* to be named, which is that there are a lot of people out there who are convinced that the decision has already been made. They believe that the discussion is a matter of going through the motions, and that the decision will then simply be announced. This is the expression of a sense of impending betrayal that needs to be dealt with, or we will experience a wholesale exodus.

JMC: Another factor in this is that, even when you are standing fast with what has been the church's consistent teaching on these issues, you are—because you are engaged in dialogue on it—already in a changed situation. You, in fact, are not going back to the way things were. You may be standing fast, but in the midst of questioning about change; whereas the way the things were before, change was not being recommended and your views were not being challenged.

MAP: I wanted to try to say a more positive word about the church because I think we are naming some negative perspectives of people who are entrenched in a particular mindset. I believe, perhaps naively, that the great majority of people in the ELCA want to do the will of God on this matter. They want to know what the Bible does say, what the leaders in the church who are entrusted to study these matters think. Some folks may be somewhat confused. They have always heard that the Bible says homosexuality is wrong. Now some people are saying that interpretation is not correct. They may also know relatives who are gay and seem like wonderful people and are good Christians, and do not understand how that can be. Those kinds of things are going on and people are sincerely looking to the church for help in figuring out what God thinks about all this. They want to know and they are empathic listeners; they do not know yet what they are going to end up believing. I think there are a lot of people like that.

RP: I would agree with Mark: that there are people who do believe that this process that we are going through is a helpful, meaningful process that will help us understand ourselves and get clarity about what we believe. I also want to be realistic and say that I have heard other folks who say that it is a forgone conclusion what the decision is going to be. I would rather not hide that fact but get it out there and talk about it and engage in the kind of conversation José was talking about, how we can have a conversation and a dialogue with each other and come to see how we are united in our baptism.

MS: What I have learned about this subject over the years—I was on the initial task force that the LCA had on this in 1985—is how stuck we are. When you talk about being a child of God, you realize that we are children of God. The one thing that is hard to do is to divorce your brothers and sisters wherever they are on this issue; it is very hard to pretend they do not exist. Some of the most interesting conversations I have had have been with persons of a very different viewpoint. We may not have changed our views much as a result, but we remain "stuck" together as sisters and brothers in Christ.

People often say that if you have the experience of a gay or lesbian person in your family, if you talk and meet gay and lesbian Christians and hear their stories, it makes a difference in your outlook toward their role in the church. This is a dimension of experience that we have only written about indirectly in this volume. What role do you think that reflection on this aspect of experience should play in the church's discussion?

DO: I think it is a necessary thing. If you are simply talking about people, you are gossiping, and there is nothing respectful about gossiping about somebody. I think we need to hear people tell us about their experience. I think we need to get to know gay and lesbian people as human beings.

RP: Two strategies, to my mind. First and foremost, I think it is necessary to have gay and lesbian persons part of the conversation as much as possible. Second, if there are not gay and lesbian persons who are willing to participate in the discussion, that changes the questions. I do not want to objectify, so I am not going to talk about them; I am going to talk about me. What are the issues that I face as a heterosexual male around this particular issue? This strategy prevents me from objectifying people who are not part of the conversation. So I think there are two strategies, depending on the situation in which I find myself. If I find I have access and can reach gay and lesbian persons, then it's necessary for them to participate in the conversation because it keeps everyone honest. But if the folks are not there, then I have to have another strategy to deal with the folks who are there who are heterosexuals.

JDR: The other problem is dealing with perceptions. I think that if we are going to have a conversation where we want ourselves to be heard, then we need to discipline ourselves in maintaining the same standard of respect toward all. I also do not think that it is sufficient to allow our perceptions of people to be unexamined as we try to resolve a matter that goes beyond our individual experience. That just reinforces stereotypes and biases and does nothing for greater clarity and the ability to deepen our understanding of the matter.

MS: I have talked to a lot of gay, lesbian, straight, and other people about sexuality, and it has made me more and more convinced that sexuality is in some ways an idol. Sexuality has become a commodity, entitlement, and idolatry. It should not be so definitive of identity as it is, but it really is. And that troubles me a lot, and I see a lot of sexual behavior that is fraught with troubles and problems. I see a lot of stuff out there going on with gays, straights, and others that I really want to challenge and question. I do not know why so many people want to go into ministry when they need so much help in this precise area. And it makes me all the more certain that we need to talk about this in connection with leaders of the church. I see a lot of people going into the leadership of the church with issues of sexuality. I would love to have some handles on it. So yes, talking with people is absolutely essential. Is it going to make you more sympathetic or more cautious, more frightened or more certain, that there needs to be some rich, thick normative talk about Christian discipleship in terms of sexual behavior?

JMC: I think one implication of what you are saying, Marty, is that when we are faced with the particularities of experiences that are presented to us, our sense of Christian compassion and simple humanity will make it extremely difficult not to respect that, not to feel what they feel, or at least empathetically to listen to them. Perhaps we will have an opposite response. Either way, as a result, we can be almost paralyzed in our ability to deliberate on what the teaching of the church should be. And we will be, as long as the discussion revolves around one's sexuality rather than one's identity in Christ as a sexual being. I do not know if we can escape that. I like the sound of it; I do not know if we can escape it.

DO: One of the reasons we cannot escape doing this is because it is really being forced on us. Last week I watched an hour-and-a-half forum on homosexuality. Ted Koppel had arranged it so that the religious opponents were caricatured. He picked people to interview that would really make anybody who was in opposition in his own viewpoint look foolish. Given that kind of aggressive approach by the media, we really do not have any option except to talk about these things.

MS: And to show that we have a different point of view entirely. I do not want the terms of the debate to be set by the secular media or by the kind of dominant secular rights.

MP: Is the question about the role of experience, in terms of what voice do gays and lesbians themselves have?

JMC: What weight should the experience of relating to gay and lesbian persons inside and outside your family carry determining our views and decisions?

MP: As Lutherans our authority does not lie in our experiences or the experience of others but in Holy Scripture, the Word of God. So there has to be a caution about experience. I think there are many in our church who are afraid that experience somehow will take precedent over what is the revealed wisdom of the ages, the Word of God, and even the tradition of the church. There is a tendency today for current experience to somehow have more authority than two thousand years of experience in the church. But I also hear people who wish to make that point sort of go overboard and say that as long as they know what the Bible says, it does not make any difference. And the testimonies of other Christians are always significant. In Acts 15, with the first big dispute the church had, Christians got together to argue about whether and under what terms Gentiles could be part of the church. Peter did not get out his Bible and start exegeting a text. He talked about the encounter he had with Cornelius, and how Cornelius had been filled with the Holy Spirit just as they had been at the day of Pentecost, and everybody seemed to think that that was an important point. I think the testimonies and observance of what the Spirit is doing in the lives of people is significant.

I should also say that I think that whatever our experiences have been, we start out at different points based on those experiences. However, I do not think that it is going to make that much difference ultimately, because I think that if we pray to God and trust in God that God is going to reveal to us the truth of what we know and what we should do, and as a church we are going to come together as a community to understand what God wants us to understand. I believe that in part because the person who had Jim Childs' job at the Council in Acts 15 was another Jim: James, the brother of our Lord Jesus Christ. In his epistle he says, "If any of you lacks wisdom, ask God, who gives to all generously . . . but ask in faith and without doubting."

Through the Spirit, through Scripture, through tradition, through reason, through whatever means necessary, I believe that God is going to show us the way that we should go and I believe that we are going to go that way.

JMC: This sounds like a good point to close on, because I think that a lot of the anxiety that one encounters in the church about what we are going to do, or how we are going to go through this thing, does not give the Holy Spirit enough credit. I think we should expect a lot from the Spirit—I do.